Noah,
We celebrate
accomplishment of college graduation.
We look forward to continuing to witness
God working in & through you.

ENTHRONED

Excellent book for Worshippers!

**BRINGING GOD'S KINGDOM TO EARTH
THROUGH UNCEASING WORSHIP & PRAYER**

Love, Doc & Mrs WINE

DAVID FRITCH -
my niece, Heather's husband

ENTHRONED

BRINGING GOD'S KINGDOM TO EARTH THROUGH UNCEASING WORSHIP AND PRAYER

Copyright 2017 David Fritch

Published by David Fritch

Cover Design by Chris Conley

Formatted for publishing by Docs2eBooks

Scripture quotes were taken from New King James Version (NKJV) unless otherwise noted.

There has never been a more important time in our history for prayer. The 24/7 houses of prayer that understand the glorious realm of worship and prayer mingled together to bring heaven to earth. I thank David and all those who have committed themselves to see, through worship, the heavenly realm of God and pray from His heart.

—**Beni Johnson**, Author of *The Happy Intercessor*

David Fritch is an amazing man of God. His passion stems from his deep revelation of the Tabernacle of David, as a model to propel people into a lifelong pursuit of the presence of God. *Enthroned* takes you not only into the history of night and day worship and prayer, but gives you practical steps that, if applied, will change your present and future walk with God. I highly recommend it!

—**Stacey Campbell**, co-author of *Praying the Bible: The Book of Prayers* and *Praying the Bible: The Pathway to Spirituality*

David has given us a timely book filled with valuable information for creative worshippers. He has mined out a treasure trove of insight and revelation. This book is important; I predict that it will be for a very long time.

—**Ray Hughes**, Selah Ministries

If you want to learn about prayer and changing nations, there is no more experienced person that I can think of than David Fritch! I have known David for 20 years now. He is a man of prayer and worship and praise and I know that anything he writes comes from a posture of humility.

—**Jason Upton**, Key of David Ministries

Amos 9:11 is not a vague or archaic prophecy from the Old Testament that we are following, but a living, vibrant and powerful force reshaping the earth. There is no one better to scribe the scope, testimony and theology of this movement other than my friend David Fritch! Dive head first into the powerful story of *Enthroned* and join the most exciting adventure in God of our generation!

—**Sean Feucht,** Founder of Burn 24-7 and Bethel Music Artist

The Tabernacle of David is both pivotal and controversial. I have been fascinated by it for more than 40 years. What is it? It is given as the explanation of the Gospel crossing the racial and cultural barrier out of a Jewish sect into a transformational missionary movement to the Nations of the Earth in Acts 15. But, what is it? No one I know has articulated this as well and as deeply as David Fritch. He gets it! He has lived it. His insights will inspire you to pursue the transformational power of the Presence! This book could change your life and might just change your world!
—**Charles Stock**,
Senior Pastor Life Center Ministries, Harrisburg PA

What makes a good book a great book is not just the information. It's also the passion of the author. David Fritch is a man of passion and prayer and his new book *Enthroned* radiates with the heart and soul of a lover of God and a lover of prayer. *Enthroned* is a must for anyone who wants to understand what God is doing today through the vehicle of worship and intercession. Thank you, David. Well done!
—**Chris DuPre**, Pastor, Speaker, and Author of *The Wild Love of God*

I have been waiting for this book for years! The depth of revelation and teaching David carries always provokes me so deeply. Truly, I believe this book will be a catalytic "unlocking" in the worship and prayer movement for an entire generation and generations to come!
—**Chris Burns**, The Sound Movement, San Francisco, and Author of *Pioneers of His Presence*

I am sure you will be blessed reading *Enthroned* as David and his team of radical burners know the secrets of how to break through even in the hell fires.
—**Karen Dunham**, Living Bread International, Jerusalem

I have seen firsthand David Fritch live out this message as we have labored together to build worship and prayer across the Middle East. God is truly doing something marvelous in our day with the convergence of the global prayer, worship and missions movement! I believe *Enthroned* will give clarity and

biblical understanding to what God is already doing in the nations and will embolden a new wave of singing missionaries to go the ends of the earth.
—**R. Martinez**, President, MAPS Global

Few people carry the level of zeal and wisdom for the subject of worship and prayer like David Fritch. For over 20 years I have watched him model a lifestyle of worship that carries the tangible presence of God into some of the darkest corners of the earth. *Enthroned* will inspire you to daily engage with God through an intimate and transformational expression of worship that releases heaven into your home, workplace, city and the nations of the earth!
—**Adam Cates**, Big House Church

David Fritch is one of the clearest emerging voices for worship, prayer, and revival. This book will become a manual for the global worship movement. It is long overdue. I highly recommend it!
—**David Bradshaw,** Director of Fredericksburg Prayer Furnace and Awaken the Dawn

Few people have had the impact on my life and placed a seed of revelation in my heart concerning the message of the Tabernacle of David like David Fritch has. Not only has he obtained great revelation, but he has always put it into action by pioneering Davidic movements of worship and prayer around the world. My heart comes alive whenever I'm around him!!
—**Jamie Dickson**, Senior Pastor, Kingdom Life Church and Burn 24-7 Northeast Regional Director

David Fritch is a true pioneer in the faith and his faithfulness to share his journey with others has been a lasting inspiration to everyone who meets him. I have had the privilege of personally watching David wrestle to accurately articulate the heart of God on so many issues and the topic of worship and prayer has been given a great deal of attention. I wholeheartedly recommend this book, and even more so, the man who has written it.
—**Tannon Herman**, Founder of Wild Heart Ministries and Author of *Time To Live.*

David has radically lived the message of this book and is an excellent communicator. Combining biblical, historical, and modern examples into one blueprint Dave has created an incredibly needed tool to multiply the lifestyle of 24/7 worship and prayer.

—**Jeremy Bardwell**, Media Director, PULSE Movement

Acknowledgments

I am overflowing with gratefulness for the contribution that **Mike Bickle** and **Lou Engle** have given to our generation in the area of prayer. They have blazed trails and given language for our generation to build the dreams of God's heart. Their teaching has been a deep well that I have drawn from over the years.

To **my wife**, the love of my life! How can I express the overwhelming gratitude I have for you? Your love, support and encouragement were the fuel that kept me going! Thanks for believing in me and sacrificing time and sleep so I could write!

I thank **my mom and dad** for giving me such a love and foundation in the Word of God. I am so thankful for the endless encouragement my mom gave me to write this book. I definitely wouldn't have had the courage to do this without her.

I am grateful to **Sean Feucht** for inspiring all of us to call the nations to worship and for giving me a context to run with my dreams.

I thank **Chris Burns** for always calling me and encouraging me at just the right time to not give up on my dream to write this book.

I thank **Chris Conley** for designing the cover and for being just as excited as I am for this book to happen!

I also thank **Sharon Threatt** for her incredible and speedy formatting work! Her insights were invaluable in helping me finish this.

To my children: The stories, revelations and encounters recorded in this book are your inheritance. My prayer is that you will start where I left off and go further and higher! You are my joy and my first and favorite ministry.

Table of Contents

BUT YOU ARE HOLY,
ENTHRONED ON THE
PRAISES OF ISRAEL.
(Psalm 22:3 NLT)

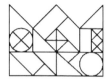

What in the World is God Doing?

It was 5:00 a.m. and our group had driven all night to make sure we could get good seats to what I thought was one of the latest hyped up Christian festivals. I was a youth pastor at the time and had been to my fair share of these events. I was beginning to question the fruitfulness of these celebrity-driven pep rallies, which seemed more about promoting names and products rather leading people to Jesus.

So, when I stepped onto the lawn of the National Mall in Washington D.C., for TheCall, hosted by Lou Engle, I wasn't prepared for what I encountered. We arrived right at dawn as the sun was slowly fading away and the first rays of golden sunlight were starting to peek over the dome of the state capitol. To my amazement several thousand people were already pressed to the front of a large stage for the pre-event worship.

As soon I heard the first raw, spontaneous eruptions from the worship team I felt translated into another realm. This wasn't just another cotton-candy Christian concert—this was a move of God! The atmosphere was absolutely electric with the presence of God and hunger for revival was palpable. I was totally undone! I felt so saturated by the Holy Spirit that I could barely stand and the actual event hadn't even started yet.

The hours passed like they were minutes and as we sang the crowds grew larger and larger. By nine in the morning there were an estimated 500,000 worshipers in attendance. The crowds were awe-inspiring, but this isn't what impressed me the most. There was an unshakable feeling that this was a destiny-defining moment. Revolution seemed to be in the very air we were breathing and a deep conviction that our prayers were changing history.

In the natural, there was nothing about this event that would have merited such a vast crowd. There weren't many speakers or singers with enough name recognition to draw a crowd of this size and yet there we were, with over half a million people! This wasn't a festival, it was a call to fast and pray for another great awakening!

I've been around a lot of loud and passionate people in my lifetime, but I have never heard prayer like I heard at TheCall. People cried out to God as if the fate of the nation depended on it. There was a timbre of groaning and travail in the voices of those who prayed. Over and over young intercessors ended up in a puddle of tears on the ground as they cried out in repentance for the sins of the nation.

At one point it began to rain and I thought for sure there would be a mass exodus. However, not one person in my line of sight left. The harder it rained, the harder we prayed. Tears often come to my eyes when I remember the thousands of young people lying in the mud, pounding the ground and crying out for revival in America. The rain couldn't put out the fire that was burning in our hearts as we prayed. I joined the prostrated masses in the mud. With mud-stained faces we sang, cried, repented, and danced for twelve hours! Seeing hundreds of thousands of believers from every race and denomination gather to humble themselves and pray, marked me forever. My eyes were opened! I saw what was coming and knew that I had to give my life to the cause of revival!

A Defining Moment

This was my introduction to the global night and day worship and prayer movement that began the year before on the eve of the new millennium. The year 1999 was a defining moment for the church. I believe we will point back to this year as the beginning of a great awakening and reformation in the church. This was the year that two very different, equally powerful, 24–7 global prayer movements had their humble, but powerful beginnings: the International House of Prayer in Kansas City, MO, led by Mike Bickle and 24-7 Prayer in the United Kingdom under the leadership of Pete Greig.

It was as if a trumpet blasted in 1999 and called the church to pray! In just a few short years this idea went viral. From the tiny prayer room started on the south coast of England, the 24-7 Prayer movement has seen over 10,000 prayer rooms launched globally. Prayer rooms inspired by this model have popped up in the most unlikely places—from the slums of New Delhi to the backrooms of pubs in North America.

24-7 Prayer focused on setting up creative and interactive spaces where worshipers could take one-hour shifts to pray around the clock. The room itself became an expression of intercession as participants wrote, drew or painted their prayers on the walls. Eventually, evangelism and justice initiatives emerged from the flames of this movement. It is now common place for 24-7 Prayer rooms to combine outreach with non stop prayer campaigns.

The International House of Prayer in Kansas grew from a handful of intercessors and musicians meeting in a trailer to a staff of over 2,000 people. In just a few years they have become the global leader in prayer, worship and missions. Thousands of students have come through their university, internship programs, and music school and are making an impact all over the world. They have produced world class music and published a host of books and resources to equip the church to pray. They innovated new models of intercession such as the "Harp and Bowl" prayer, which is a creative blending of prayer with spontaneous and responsive singing. Thousands of groups across the world, inspired by their story, have launched their own version of the 24-7 House of Prayer.

Other movements have come and gone but these two seemed to have a catalytic quality to them. It was as if the fullness of time had come for the 24-7 House of Prayer. Following the trail these early pioneers blazed, people began to meet in homes, storefronts, stadiums, college dorms, and even prisons to cry out to God for revival. These movements validated and brought to the forefront the role of the intercessor as a full-time occupation and hundreds left their jobs to live by faith and pray and fast full time. Entire churches closed and converted into houses of prayer. The idea transcended denominational boundaries as both mainline denominational churches and charismatic congregations began to open 24-7 prayer rooms.

Prior to 1999 in America only a handful of ministries had pursued night and day worship and prayer, but today there are thousands! While writing this, I did a google search using the term "24-7 prayer" and over 750,000 websites came up. I also entered the phrase "house of prayer" which yielded 30 million websites. We are in an unprecedented explosion of prayer in the earth.

I believe the prayer movement is a sign and wonder in and of itself. John Wesley, founder of the Methodist church, said, "God never does anything in the earth except through believing prayer." The implications of this statement are staggering! What will it look like for God to answer years of persistent night and day worship and prayer? I'm not sure we even have a historic precedent to show us what it will be like. In the end, I believe it will result in radical revival, reformation of the church and billions of souls coming to the Lord!

A Divine Intersection

A few years after my experience at TheCall DC, my life divinely intersected with a grassroots 24-7 worship and prayer movement called Burn 24-7. Under the leadership of Sean Feucht, this fledgling movement started as a dorm-room worship gathering on Oral Roberts University Campus and exploded into a citywide worship gathering within months. They were organizing 24-, 36-, and 48-hour worship events that would move from church to church. Dividing walls were falling and the pulse of revival was being felt all over the city. This idea soon went viral as people started using this model for worship and prayer all over the world. These groups became known as Burn Furnaces. Today there are over 250 Burn Furnaces worldwide.

When I first heard about the Burn it was a massive turning point for me. I honestly thought God had dropped me on the backside of the desert and left me to die. I was serving as an associate pastor at a church in the small town of Shawnee, Oklahoma right in the heart of the Bible belt. It was an amazing church, but I honestly felt like we spent most of our time trying to compete with the rapidly growing multi-campus mega churches spreading across central Oklahoma. I was weary from hours of unending meetings about how to retain visitors, how to break attendance barriers, and how to keep the worship music contemporary enough to draw the young ones, but not too wild to scare off the older folks. My encounter at TheCall ruined me for ordinary church life! I wanted revival more than anything.

When I heard the testimonies coming out of the Burn in Tulsa it called to a deep place in my heart. There was a raw, authentic cry of desperation for revival pouring out from the Burn 24-7 that compelled me. No one around me talked about revival and most of the churches I visited had empty prayer rooms. When I met people from the Burn I felt like I had met my tribe—people who got it! We spoke the same language and had the same heart cry for awakening. It wasn't long before I joined the ranks of the Burn 24-7 and helped pioneer the fourth Burn Furnace in the movement's short existence.

I seriously felt alone in my calling to pioneer night and day worship and prayer until God divinely connected me with a young worship leader named Ryan. Ryan and his wife Kristy had been praying for revival in Shawnee years before I ever moved there. We had an instant connection and knew God had called us as a team to plant the town's first 24-7 prayer expression. We prayed, fasted, and shared our vision with worship leaders and pastors all over the city for months. We finally found a pastor courageous enough to open his doors for our first 24-hour Burn Event. Later, this pastor confessed to us that he had no idea what we were trying to do, but let us use his church because he loved our passion.

On the day of our first Burn Event we had no idea if anyone would show up. To our amazement over one hundred and fifty people attended! We discovered that hidden away in this little town there were others praying, believing and longing for revival just like us. These hungry, frustrated, broken and desperate intercessors and prophets came out of the woodwork to pray all night long. Some were so hungry that many stayed the entire twenty-four hours. The presence of God hung like a thick fog over that place the entire weekend.

On Saturday morning of the event a whole group of grey-headed ladies filled the back row of the church. I was a bit concerned because they walked in right at the moment an energetic youth band was literally screaming and pulling out all the stops on their electric guitars. I thought for sure they would leave within minutes, but to my surprise their hands went up and they began to sway and move to the music. It was clear they loved Jesus and weren't afraid to show it! They must have stayed for at least six hours. I kept thinking, "Who are these women? Where did they come from?"

I had to meet these amazing mothers in the faith. I approached one of the ladies and she literally grabbed me by the collar and with tear-stained eyes said, "This is God! Don't ever stop doing this. Our group of ladies are part of a Baptist church and we have been praying for revival in this town for over twenty-five years! You are an answer to our prayers." These little Baptist ladies became some of our biggest supporters and attended almost every event we ever held. For the next seven years we hosted nonstop worship events in churches, homeless shelters, parks and homes! People were healed and revived month after month and denominational barriers fell as the church united in an unprecedented way. Missions and evangelism efforts exploded from our little furnace as short-term teams were sent from Shawnee to the nations.

In 2007, a radical group of young people found each other in the nightwatch. As they cried out to God for revival they got a wild vision to take a bus across America to worship, pray for revival and preach the gospel. This group became known as the Burn Wagon. On their first trip they took thirty young people in an 1970 Greyhound bus up and down the east coast of America. They worshipped at parks, shopping centers and any church that would open their doors for a service. Everywhere they went they planted seeds of revival. Since then, Burn Wagon teams have traveled coast to coast every summer for over ten years in the United States, as well as Europe and Canada! Hundreds of people have been saved and healed from the overflow of one group of praying churches in a small Oklahoma town!

A Movement Goes Viral

The same year we started our Burn Furnace others were doing the same. Word was getting out and the testimonies were spreading! Inspired by the stories of the Burn 24-7 people started planting Burn Furnaces in their cities. In our city alone, people drove for hours to see what God was doing. In early 2007 there were only four Burn Furnaces, but by the end of the year there were close to thirty. I had never been a part of something that caught fire so quickly!

Out of pure and undefiled passion for God's presence, an organic network of relationships was built over night. It felt like family—everyone wanted the same thing and talked the same language. Every time a new Burn Furnace started we would drive for hours to help each other out. There were no big names and no one was getting paid. People traveled at their own expense to steward the bonfires of prayer exploding in America.

Some left full-time jobs and ministries to pursue this holy occupation. Others pioneered storefront prayer rooms, became full-time missionaries in unreached nations and started training programs. In the very first year of the Burn, global missions became an important part of the DNA. We weren't content praying for the nations from the safety and comfort of our prayer rooms, we sent teams to the toughest places on earth just to worship and pray. Short-term teams led to long-term ventures in places like Indonesia, Nepal, Turkey and Iraq. We were convinced that our prayers were blazing trails for the gospel everywhere we went. It wasn't long before stories of supernatural encounters, breakthroughs, and salvations started flooding in. God was moving in crazy ways, but most of us had no language or Biblical understanding for what God was doing.

Amos 9:11 became our anthem. In our zeal we proclaimed that what we were doing was the restoration of the Tabernacle of David. However, almost no one in Burn 24-7 movement could really back this up scripturally. A common battle cry in those days was, "We have no idea what we are doing, but this is God!" There was something really raw and beautiful about not having it all figured out! It kept us humble and reaching out for more of God. I think God loved our youthful zeal!

Revelation on the Run

Our theology was immature, but our hearts were pure. God didn't wait to use us until our theology was ironed out—He taught us as we went. We'd have some of the most insane experiences and encounters and then God would give us understanding for it later. It reminds me how it happened in the early church. The Holy Spirit dropped like a bomb in Jerusalem as thousands were getting swept into the kingdom of God. Miracles and signs and wonders were happening everywhere they went and yet none of the New Testament had been written yet. God was moving and they didn't have a systematic theology for it. They experienced God and then He taught them. In fact, God would often confront false theology by sending an encounter first.

In the time of the Book of Acts, there was a commonly held belief that salvation was for the Jews only. The Gentiles were considered heathen and not worthy of saving. God wanted to reach the whole wide world, so what did He do? He sovereignly poured out the Holy Spirit on the Gentiles and left the church to grapple with it! The idea that God would do this blew their minds. It sparked much debate as people wrestled to figure out what God was up to. In the end, the lights came on! They started to make connections between Old Testament prophecy and the outpouring of the Spirit on the Gentiles. God taught them truth in the midst of revival. I'd say this is the best place to learn!

This was the way most New Testament theology developed. I call it "revelation on the run", because most of It was written as they traveled, doing the works of the Kingdom. What God taught them in the midst of an outpouring became the theological bedrock the next generation built upon. We need to become comfortable with knowing God often works first and then teaches second.

In the early days of the Burn we experienced this "revelation on the run." Most of the time, our encounters came first and our insight second. After a few years into the Burn I began to hear some of the most profound teaching and preaching on worship and prayer I had ever heard. These messages weren't empty echoes of other men's teachings, but living revelations born in the fires of a move of God. These early teachings became the building blocks of the Burn 24-7.

There was a time when we had no idea what we were doing or how to explain it Biblically and that was okay. However, to stay there would have stunted the growth of our movement. Legacy belongs to those who have language. What do I mean by this? If we are going to lead the next generation into what God is doing, then we must develop Biblical language and understanding for what we believe. What if the Apostle Paul had not mined out and wrote down the rich theology of the New Testament? His writings fed, nurtured and built the church generations beyond his day.

The purpose of revival is to uncover Biblical truths to which we have become blind or hardened against. Think about the Azusa Street Revival in Los Angeles at the turn of twentieth century. God unveiled the truth of the Baptism of the Holy Spirit to a new generation. Millions received a fresh baptism of power and love at Azusa Street! Over a hundred years later, thousands of groups trace their lineage back to this revival. This movement had longevity and shaped the culture of the church worldwide in large part because early pioneers mined out simple language for the doctrine of the Baptism of the Spirit.

Biblical language, born from the flames of revival, is a doorway into an encounter with God. Those who get language become the architects of Kingdom culture and movements. It's only when we clearly articulate and define what we believe, that we can disciple and call others into what God is doing.

Enthroned is a collection of my "revelations on the run!" It is the culmination of my experiences of pioneering 24-7 worship and prayer in the nations for over ten years. Many of the things I will share with you came from encounters I had sitting on prayer room floors in places like China, Iraq, Turkey, Las Vegas, and San Francisco. This book isn't a compilation of theories or nice ideas, but of truths that have been tested and tried in the furnace of pioneering.

Enthroned is a study of the Tabernacle of David and its connection to global revival and harvest. We will explore questions like, "What is the Tabernacle of David? Is the modern day prayer movement the restoration of David's Tabernacle? Was David's Tabernacle literally 24-7? What is the role of worship and prayer in the great commission? What is the believer's role in preparing for revival and harvest?"

My prayer is that you will have a living encounter with truth as you read this book; that this book will be theology on fire. I pray that you find your call, hear your marching orders and become empowered to fulfill your destiny. My desire for this book is that it will both expand your vision and give you practical tools for building the Kingdom of God in the earth.

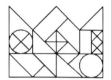

Chapter 2

AMOS 9:11 IN 3-D

"On that day I will raise up the tabernacle of David,
which has fallen down, and repair its damages; I will
raise up its ruins, and rebuild it as in the days of old;
that they may possess the remnant of Edom, and all
the Gentiles who are called by My name," says the
Lord who does this thing (Amos 9:11–12).

I scrambled to find a mental box to place this strange phrase in, but I couldn't find one. I filtered the words through my theological data bank but this only caused more confusion. So, I listened politely, but I knew I was going to have to process what I was hearing. With eyes tightly shut, and with a passionate, booming voice, my friend repeated the words of his prophecy over me, "God's going to use you to raise up a modern-day Tabernacle of David Movement." My inward dialogue went something like this, "What in the world is the Tabernacle of David? Is that even a Biblical concept? Mmm...maybe my friend is having an off day today."

I had some vague idea that the prophetic word was referring to worship and prayer, but I honestly couldn't tell you why I thought that or even where the phrase "Tabernacle of David" was in the Bible. I found this passage in the book of Amos 9:11–12 but was even more confused after I read it. I trusted that my friend's intentions were to encourage me, but since I couldn't connect to it, I put it on the shelf.

At the time I would have never imagined that this verse would become one of the defining themes of my life and ministry. Years later when I got involved in the Burn 24-7, I kept hearing the leaders talk about how the 24-7 prayer movement was the fulfillment of the Amos 9:11 prophecy which says, "On that day I will raise up the tabernacle of David which has fallen down."

In my heart I knew that the night and day worship and prayer movement I was part of was a valid move of the Holy Spirit. I also firmly believed that worship and prayer were Biblical concepts and that Jesus was worthy being glorified twenty-four hours a day. However, as a seminary graduate and a person who has a high value for Biblical accuracy, I just didn't feel comfortable making the claim that the Tabernacle of David equaled the modern day 24-7 worship and prayer movement.

Charismatic View

The more involved I became in the prayer movement, the more I discovered that most of my friends took the typical charismatic viewpoint on the Tabernacle of David. This view goes something like this: The Tabernacle of David refers to the system of 24-7 worship and prayer that King David set up on Mt. Zion. Usually after a brief conversation with those who believe this, I discovered that most of them have little to no real, firsthand Biblical insight on the matter. It seemed like everyone repeated key ideas and concepts from popular teachers in the movement, but very few actually knew what the scriptures taught on this subject.

My head and heart were in a massive wrestling match. When I heard people talk about the Tabernacle of David and 24-7 prayer my heart would explode, but my head would check my heart with all the theological arguments. I really wanted to believe this viewpoint! It sure would have provided some credibility to the fledgling night and day worship movement I was involved in, but I couldn't with any honesty or authenticity agree with this viewpoint.

In private I would often criticize Charismatics for their shallow, zealous interpretations of scripture, but when I finally got real with myself, I realized I was guilty of the very same thing! Sadly, I discovered that my conclusions on this subject weren't based on a thorough firsthand study of scripture, but rather on a few commentaries and articles I read from highly respected evangelical scholars.

Evangelical View

Most evangelical scholars make no connection between the term Tabernacle of David and worship and prayer. The consensus from this community is that the term Tabernacle of David was a way to refer to the house or kingdom of David. The conclusion from this community is that the promise of restoration pointed to the coming reign of Jesus, the son of David, who would sit on his throne and restore the kingdom. Ultimately, this prophecy spoke of the advent of the kingdom of God through Jesus. As I studied this, I definitely saw that the evidence for this was stacked in their favor.

Here I was in the middle of a rapidly growing movement that boldly declared on their website that they were a part of the modern-day restoration of the Tabernacle of David and I didn't believe it. For my own heart and peace of mind I knew that I needed to move past my biases on the subject and actually see what the Bible said on the matter.

I dove into a study of the Book of Amos and what I discovered was eye-opening and became the bedrock for all future teaching on this subject. What began as a quest for Biblical accuracy ended in a full-blown encounter with truth that changed my life forever.

Diving In

I immediately started a thorough word-by-word study of the iconic prayer movement verse to see if the passage itself had a direct connection to the Davidic worship revolution.

Verse 11— "On that day I will raise up **the tabernacle of David**, which has **fallen down**, and repair its damages; I will **raise up its ruins**, and **rebuild it** as in the days of old;

Verse 12— that they may possess the remnant of Edom, and all the Gentiles who are called by My name," says the LORD who does this thing (Amos 9:11-12) (emphasis mine).

Defining the Terms

First, it's clear from the context that Amos used the term Tabernacle of David to refer to the nation of Israel as a whole. The Hebrew word used here for Tabernacle is *sukka*. *Sukka* literally means "booth" or "shelter" and refers to temporary, makeshift shelters made of branches and leaves. During Amos' time this word was used in one of two contexts: It referred to cattle shelters, or the temporary shanties the Israelites constructed to celebrate the Feast of Tabernacles.

So, why did Amos call Israel the "shelter of David"? In this passage, Amos describes Israel as fallen down, damaged, and in ruins. The original readers would have thought this idea was absolutely ridiculous. In the natural they were at the peak of their prosperity and military victory—they were nowhere near to a state of ruins. However, Amos wasn't talking about the outward measurements of success, but instead, the state of their hearts. Verse eleven is basically a summary of the first eight chapters of the book, which is an exposé of the sins of the nation.

Calling them the *sukka* of David was meant to expose their true spiritual condition and cut them to the heart. The original readers would have got the message loud and clear. He was basically telling them, "You think you are an invincible empire, but you are actually nothing more than a broken down shanty that is vulnerable to the lightest breeze."

The Context

When I read the first eight chapters of Amos, I was blown away. Amos was no light-weight prophet. He was fierce and fearless and held nothing back in his confrontation of the nation. The oracles of this unknown shepherd-prophet from the hills of Tekoa seemed to pierce the air like a knife when I read them. With the precision of a master swordsmen, he laid Israel bare with the sword of truth. Amos preached hellfire and brimstone to a nation that had fallen headlong into blatant idolatry, were divided and at war with one another, and had justified exploitation of the poorest of poor. Here are just a few of their transgressions:

- **Civil War**: Israel had been ripped into two nations, with ten northern tribes identifying as Israel and two southern tribes identifying as Judah. Leading up to this writing, God's people had deep roots of bitterness and hatred that frequently led to civil war and the slaughtering of their own people.

- **They despised God's Word**: "Because they have despised the law of the Lord and have not kept His commandments" (Amos 2:4). Now it's one thing to just ignore the Word of God, but to despise God's Word is an indication of massive spiritual coldness and hardness of heart. When you read the following sins you realize that rejecting the Word of God is really the original sin.

- **Sold their brothers into slavery**: "…because they sell the righteous for silver" (Amos 2:6). How far gone do you have to be to degrade human life to slavery…and not just any human life, but your own people? Their greed and perversion were completely out of control.

- **Dehumanizing and exploitation of the poor**: They had become so greedy and had so dehumanized the poor that they sold them for the price of a sandal—mere pennies.

- **Sexual perversion**: They were guilty of incest and sleeping with ritual prostitutes at the temple of God. How far gone were they that they had justified such perversion in places consecrated to the pure worship of God?

- **Blatant idolatry**: They set up altars to false gods in all the holy places and integrated pagan worship with the worship of God. The crazy part is that they continued to pay their tithe and offer sacrifices to God while worshipping Baal (Amos 4:4–5).

A Ray of Hope

These were the sons of David, fallen, broken and in desperate need of revival! They were but a shadow of their former glory, but God wasn't finished with them yet. After eight chapters of doom, gloom and judgment we finally see a ray of hope, a glimpse into the bright and glorious future. Amos 9:11 isn't just an exposé of their past, but it's a glimpse into their bright future. The Word of the Lord didn't come to Israel to crush them and cast them out. It was meant as a divine wake-up call and to provoke them to thirst for God again. In light of their degraded and fallen state it's absolutely stunning that God gave them such glorious promises—and not just any promises—He gave them the Messianic seed! In the midst of their rebellion they became the doorway to a Word that would shift human history forever.

Disappointment

I loved studying the book of Amos, but I was left feeling disappointed. I combed through this book verse by verse and couldn't find any direct connection between the Tabernacle of David and night and day worship and prayer. It confirmed my original thinking that the Tabernacle of David primarily fore-shadowed the Messianic reign when Jesus took leadership of the House of David. However, I couldn't shake the sense that God still wanted to teach me something about this subject. I determined to remain a student of the Word and keep my heart open.

The Bible in 3-D

When I was a kid I remember walking by a store in the mall where a group of people were staring intently at a large poster. I was curious, so I joined them. One by one the people began to exclaim, "I see it! Do you see it? I see it! There it is...dolphins swimming." I was eager to see what the excitement was all about, but when I looked all I saw was a series of pixelated images...visual gibberish, really. One of the onlookers explained that it was a magic eye picture and that if you stared at it just the right way you would see a 3-D image pop out before your eyes.

I stood there for over fifteen minutes as person after person saw the hidden image within seconds of focusing on it...yet, I still couldn't see it. I was frustrated but determined to see the magic. After almost giving up, an eight-year-old kid gave me a tip that finally gave me the breakthrough. He said, "You have to look past the picture and slightly cross your eyes." Well, it sounded weird, but I gave it a shot! There it was! Right before my eyes, almost floating in the air, were the mystical neon-colored flying dolphins.

My study of the book of Amos sort of felt like my 1980's experience of staring at the magic eye poster. I studied and studied Amos and couldn't see it until a friend gave me the key that helped me see this scripture in 3-D. After a couple of hours of talking about what God is doing in the earth through night and day worship and prayer, our conversation led to the theology of it. I shared with my friend my conclusions and questions regarding Amos 9:11. He made a passing comment that floored me! It was the key that opened my heart to a whole new realm of insight and revelation. It clearly wasn't a revolutionary statement to my friend, but to me it was the moment the lights turned on, a moment of clarity and insight that unlocked this passage.

He said, "It's true the term Tabernacle of David refers to the Davidic Kingdom, but worship and prayer were the very foundation and heart of everything he did. You really can't separate the two." That was it! There it was! Could it be that both interpretations of the Tabernacle of David were right and that they fit together like a beautiful puzzle?

I left our conversation with a zeal to study the life and Kingdom of David with fresh eyes. What made David's kingdom so powerful? Why did God choose to revive David's Kingdom and not another? What were the heart and principles that David governed by? Why is David's Kingdom going to be restored? Was 24-7 worship and prayer really a part of what David did? If so, why? And how did it function?

Chapter 3

THE REVOLUTIONARY KINGDOM OF DAVID

David was born into one of the darkest times in Israel's history. To say Israel needed revival would have been an understatement. They needed a full-blown overhaul, a dismantling of corrupt systems and reformation at every level. The spiritual leadership of the nation were steeped in immorality, corruption and exploited the system to fuel their own greed. The entire government was in complete disarray as its judges "turned aside after dishonest gain, took bribes, and perverted justice" (1 Samuel 8:3). This was just the leadership!

The people of God themselves had forgotten the ancient path that had led them to greatness. The days of miracles, manna falling from heaven, rivers rolling back and the visible glory of God resting over the nation were but vague memories— bedtime stories at best. So, it's no surprise that Israel actually did what they did.

A National Falling Away

"Give us a king to judge us" they demanded (1 Samuel 8:6). I can only imagine how grieved and hurt the Prophet Samuel was when he heard this. This was nothing less than a national rejection of God. It must have cut Samuel to the heart and felt so personal to have the very people that he prophesied to, wept over and fought for from the time of his youth, abandon his God.

God comforted Samuel by telling him, "They have not rejected you, but they have rejected me that I should not reign over them" (1 Samuel 8:7). Samuel warned them of the coming deluge of evil and oppression that would be unleashed as a result of their decision. He told them that things would get so bad that they would "cry out in that day because of your king whom you have chosen for yourselves, and the Lord will not hear you in that day" (1 Samuel 8:18). Yet, they still had the courage to reject God and when they did the soul of the nation began to die.

I can't even imagine how it grieved the heart of God. Israel was unlike any other nation on the planet. The uncreated God of the universe chose them above all other people to live and dwell among. They were God's treasured possession (Exodus 19:5) and He and He alone was their King. He manifested Himself to them in glory clouds, led them by supernatural pillars of fire, and spoke to them through the prophets. This is how God led His people and as long as they honored and obeyed His word, He extravagantly blessed them. Rejecting God was the most foolish and hard-hearted thing they could have ever done.

It wasn't long before the dark clouds of fear, control and death began to rule the land and the very soul of the nation slowly began to wither. This one, seemingly small, decision opened the door to untold rebellion, depravity and darkness that enslaved the very nation whose destiny was to reign with God.

What's shocking is that God gave them exactly what they asked for. Saul, a broken, frail and prideful man replaced the glorious God of the universe as king. I love the mercy and sovereignty of God expressed in this story. Even though God's own people turned on Him, He still made an agreement with Saul that if he would listen and obey His word and humbly submit to His leadership, that all would go well with both him and the nation (1 Samuel 12:14-15). God was willing to work within the structure man had created. In order for Saul to successfully serve as a co-ruler with God, it would require a high level of humility. This is where the story goes from bad to worse. Saul made two decisions that led to the darkest days of Israel.

God's Word Rejected

Saul tasted just enough success for it to go to his head. He yielded to the deception that comes with pride and actually reached the point where he thought he knew better than God. He rebelled against the words of the prophet Samuel not once, but twice. This decision cost him and the nation dearly and from that day on Samuel never returned to prophesy to him again.

In a single moment Israel was cut off from their greatest resource—God's word. This was the very key to their success and prosperity! They were cast out of the light and forced to grope around in darkness for an entire generation. In the void of revelation Saul turned to the demonic realm for insight and eventually became totally and utterly demonized. He rejected God's holy word in favor of demonic counsel. His pride opened the door for Satan to take a seat of authority that was never meant to be. What kind of nefarious schemes and plans were unleashed to bind and enslave God's chosen people? Israel came under the tyranny of a demonized king who would go to any lengths—including murder—to enforce his will. Can you imagine what life was like? The real tragedy of this story is that an entire generation grew up without the voice of God to comfort, strengthen and guide them.

God's Presence Neglected

Not only did Saul lead Israel into a national rebellion against the Word of the Lord, he completely and utterly abandoned the presence of God. The Ark of the Covenant was the place where heaven met earth. David referred to it as the footstool of God (1 Chronicles 28:2). Wherever the Ark was, God promised to manifest His glory and presence. The Ark was the single most important thing that Israel possessed. It gave them their identity as a people. They were called out, above all the nations to host the very presence of God in the earth. His presence was their lifeblood, it was their most valuable resource. It was the ecosystem that caused them to soar to heights of greatness and become legends to the surrounding nations. It's absolutely stunning to think that God would dwell on earth with men, but this was His deepest desire. To abandon the Ark, was to abandon His life-giving presence.

Yet the Ark sat, undesired, and unpursued for forty years. Where was the hunger? Where was the desire for God? There is no greater delusion than what pride brings. Pride nurtures the myth of self-sufficiency; it gives you the false sense of security that you can live life outside of His presence. Yet, His presence is the air we breathe—we cannot live without Him. Pride deceives us and ultimately it kills our appetite for God. The leader of God's people was both prideful and independent. He didn't want God; he didn't think he needed God and so the Ark sat in the wilderness of Kiriath Jearim for an entire generation (1 Samuel 7:2).

The tragedy of this story was that God's chosen family was cut off from the life-giving flow of His presence. They traded the presence of the King of Glory for a weak, frail, demon-possessed man who led the nation into a destructive downward spiral. These were some of the darkest days in Israel's history. This was, indeed, a generation in need of a massive spiritual awakening and a governmental reformation. Yet, this was the generation where David found his sound!

A Sound from the Hidden Places

Reformers find their cause in the midst of the darkest moral and spiritual climates. Spiritual poverty creates the necessary conditions to provoke hope-filled dreamers to leave the status quo and courageously build a better tomorrow. Right in the midst of a nation being ripped to shreds by rogue powers and principalities, a new sound was being forged in the heart of a young shepherd boy on the hillside Judah.

In the underground, far removed from power-hungry politicians and greedy priests, David fell in love with his God. His simple songs of love and hunger for God were counter-cultural to the core. As the nation grew colder and colder towards God, the fire of David's passion for God only intensified. In his unwavering pursuit of God, he both resisted the spiritual indifference of his people and caught the attention of heaven.

This was the kind of man God wanted for king—hungry and humble. There was a stark contrast between the heart of David and the heart of Saul. Saul may have thought he rejected God, but in the end God rejected him and chose a man after His own heart.

David's love for God ripped through forty years of rebellion and compelled him to establish a new and holy order in Israel. David didn't just become the next king, he became the architect of the very Kingdom of God on earth.

David's Revolutionary First Move

In America, what a president chooses as his first political move is by far the most important. The first move can make or break an administration. Much thought is given to these initial decisions because they have the potential to inspire confidence and create positive forward momentum throughout a president's tenure.

David's first act as king was absolutely revolutionary and must have shocked all who looked on. I can imagine him sitting around the boardroom with his advisors discussing what their first move would be. One may have said, "We should invest in and expand our military. We must secure our borders." Who wouldn't have agreed with that kind of practical wisdom? Another may have suggested, "We should review and reform our economic policies." Who wouldn't want greater economic stability and an increase of prosperity?

All of these ideas would have been logical and extremely practical, but David knew that it would take more than logic to incite a revolution—it would take a God-sized dream. David knew that he could not turn the hearts of a cold-hearted people back to God with spreadsheets and a five-year plan. His first move was neither logical or practical in any sense, but it was exploding with passion—and passion often looks crazy to an apathetic culture.

I can imagine the eager anticipation in the room and the jaws that dropped when David finally revealed his master plan. David may have said something like this, "Here's what we are going to do: We are going to get God in our midst again. We are going to rescue the Ark of the Covenant from the wilderness, put it under a tent without a veil, right next to our headquarters on Mt. Zion and hire 4,288 full-time singers and musicians to worship the Lord twenty-four hours a day. And by the way it's going to cost about one billion dollars."

Silence. Shock. Questioning. More questioning.

"Wait...we are going to do what? This is the strategy? But why?"

David's decision wasn't born of youthful zeal, but from a deep well of love for God that had been tested and tried through decades of hardship and persecution. He led from the wisdom of heaven and under the spirit of prophecy. David inaugurated one of the greatest reformations of all time. He dismantled every decision and system that had sprung up from the ungodly soil of Saul's heart and established Israel back on the foundations of the Kingdom of Heaven. David's leadership style was the exact opposite of King Saul. David brought the people of God into alignment with the value system of heaven and the results were astounding. Let's take a closer look at this great reformation and the values that David restored back to the land.

David Crowned God King

In David's youth, Israel turned their back on God as the King. He saw firsthand the devastation of this model. When man is at the center it always breeds pride, rebellion, and control. David knew that there is absolutely no success unless God is at the center. So, David's first and primary act was to give the crown back to God. Psalm 24 was composed to be sung as they brought up the Ark of the Covenant to Mt. Zion. This was God's coronation day! This was the day that David reversed the curse brought on the land by Israel's refusal of God's leadership. The people of God carried the Ark on their shoulders, in similar fashion to the ancient kings that were carried on a palanquin.

Can you imagine the thoughts and feelings that coursed through David's heart as he stood at the foot of Mt. Zion? This was the dawn of a whole new era! On this day the sting of years of hardship and persecution would end. On this day the emptiness and void felt in the land because of the exile of the King of Glory would end. On this day the dream of David's heart to live life in God's presence would be fulfilled. This would be the moment that light would shine and a new generation would rise to crown the King of Glory ruler over the nation again.

As they approached the Mountain of the Lord, the cry came from the singers, "Lift up your heads, O you gates! And be lifted up, you everlasting doors! And the King of glory shall come in" (Psalm 24:7). This was a prophetic call and an invitation for Israel to open the gates to the King of Glory that had previously been slammed shut.

David had the simple but profound revelation that God was "enthroned on the praises of His people" (Psalm 22:3). So David brought the Ark up to Zion, the governmental center of the nation and built a throne of unceasing worship and prayer for thirty-three years! The songs and prayers going up on the Hill of the Lord rang out over the land as a continual reminder that they served the King of Glory. The sound of His name would literally be heard night and day as they went about their business and conducted governmental affairs. This was an extravagant demonstration of humility and dependence on God to lead and guide them. As God was given His rightful place as King over the nation, Israel became God's kingdom on earth.

The presence of God was his political strategy. It was his governmental platform and foundation. He knew the presence of God was the solution to a nation in crisis. When David brought up the Ark, he was giving the crown back to God and declaring Him the rightful King of Israel. This was government as God had always intended it. He established a government of humility that was dependent upon and revolved around the presence of God.

The Heart of David

David was a worshiper before He became King; this was the driving force behind everything he did. Before he was given a title or had any political or international influence he was a shepherd boy singing simple songs of devotion on the hillsides of Judah. He encountered God in profound ways and penned some of the deepest theology of the heart of God of all time.

I wonder if David ever dreamt that his private worship songs and poems would become national anthems? His pursuit of God was Israel's national treasure. David's deep love for God provoked his people to thirst for God. He lived what He sang and invited all who heard to do the same. His yearning for God's presence defined him, radically altered his value system and influenced every decision he ever made.

Psalm 27:4 is the cry of David's heart and the foundation stone of David's Tabernacle:

> One thing I have desired of the Lord
> That will I seek:
> That I may dwell in the house of the Lord
> All the days of my life,
> To behold the beauty of the Lord,
> And to inquire in His temple.

When David erected a tent for night and day worship on Mt. Zion he was inviting the entire nation into the face-to-face encounter that he enjoyed as a shepherd on the hillside. It was as if he was simply saying, "I've seen Him and He's good and beautiful and I want all of my friends and countrymen to know Him, too. There was no veil, no restrictions to God's presence—all had access. He called his people back to their true identity.

A Return to the Priestly Calling

On his coronation day David made an extremely bold statement that would, no doubt, be burned into the national consciousness for generations to come. Saul was extreme in his rebellion, but David was equally extreme in his humility. He refused the robe of the king and traded it for the linen ephod of a priest and danced like a wild man before the Lord. He identified himself not with the tyrannical, power-hungry authority figures of his day, but with the penniless and humble priesthood whose sole inheritance was the presence of God. His declaration was clear: "There will only be one King over the land and all else must bow low and worship."

David wasn't from the priestly lineage and actually had no right to put on the priestly vestments. This would've been both shocking and offensive to many. However, this wasn't arrogance or presumption, but a revelation of God's original intention for Israel to be a "kingdom of priests and a holy nation" (Exodus 19:6). This was a powerful prophetic act. It was as if David was shouting over his people, "This is who you are! This is what you were made for!" In David's time, the priests were the only ones who had access to the holy of holies—to the very presence of God. But God never intended this. The ancient call of every man was to live life in the presence of God. What David realized, in part, was actually a prophetic word about the coming Christ who would rip the veil and give all access to His presence again.

Restoration of the Prophetic

In his arrogance, Saul turned a deaf ear to the prophetic word of the Lord, but David pursued the word of the Lord above all else. He made the prophetic ministry a core value and part of the governmental operations. He appointed three prophets to the top tier of his leadership team. "Moreover, David and the captains of the army separated for the service some of the sons of Asaph, of Heman, and of Jeduthun, who should prophesy with harps, stringed instruments, and cymbals" (1 Chronicles 25:1). Their job was to create an atmosphere and context where the prophetic ministry could function at its highest.

David ripped the ceiling off the prophetic ministry and the Word of the Lord flowed like a river from Mt. Zion. His Word washed them, healed them and elevated them to an unparalleled position of favor and influence. For thirty-three years Israel experienced a direct connection to the throne room of God and heard and saw things hundreds of years beyond their day. Scribes would sit in the Tabernacle of David and record the prophetic utterances and songs, many of which were included in the book of Psalms. Some of these songs were prophetic glimpses into the coming Messiah. Think about it! They were speaking, declaring and singing about things that would not happen for hundreds of years. They were being caught up into the realm without time to see God's glorious, unfolding plan of redemption. They sang the future and destiny of nations from that tiny hillside in the Middle East. David expressed his humble dependence on God by honoring the prophetic ministry. He knew that his real success was in both hearing and obeying God's voice.

Partnership with God

David's Tabernacle is a model for how God works with mankind to extend the borders of His Kingdom in the earth. It's an incredible thought, but God gave dominion over the earth to human beings. Beside the Godhead, we have the highest level of authority in earth. As God's representatives, our decisions carry incredible weight and significance for what happens in the earth. We have the power to choose whether evil or righteousness will rule the land. The enemy can only rule when men surrender their power by agreeing with him. Whoever we agree with, we empower. Whoever we exalt, we enthrone. If we don't want God among us, He will not come. If we choose to give our allegiance to works of darkness, He will allow it. God chooses to cooperate with the governmental structure He set in place. He will not override the will of man just to enforce His.

This makes what David did all the more powerful! Through night and day worship and prayer, David established a place of continual agreement with the will of God in the earth. David knew they weren't just singing songs, but were building a throne and habitation for the King of Kings to rule the land again. As they sang, God fought! As they cast their crowns down, God took up His. As they bowed down, God rose victorious over all their enemies!

The impact of creating a place of continuous agreement with God were stunning! God gave David unprecedented military victory and abundant wealth. War and poverty were literally obliterated in David's day. When David passed away, he left to his son Solomon the incredible and extravagant inheritance of peace and prosperity. In just one generation Israel rose from a rogue tribal people to a global superpower. Under Solomon's reign, the nations streamed to Zion to drink of the wealth, wisdom and creativity that poured from the throne of God.

A Kingdom Movement

King David was a counter-cultural revolutionary! He led a subversive singing movement, defied the tyranny of a forty-year rebellion against God and called down the godless, humanistic systems propagated by King Saul. He sparked an unprecedented spiritual awakening and a governmental reformation when he made night and day worship and prayer the driving force of the nation.

Yet, David's Tabernacle wasn't a worship and prayer movement as much as it was a Kingdom movement. David gave us a clear picture of what the Kingdom of God is like and how God works with man to expand its borders. David modeled the heart, values and principles of God's Kingdom. David's legacy to all future generations are the prophetic blueprints for bringing heaven on earth. This is the Kingdom that's rising! This is the Kingdom that Amos promised would be restored in the last days.

Chapter 4

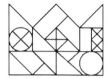

THE PATTERN OF HEAVEN

Was David crazy or inspired? Why in the world would he spend millions of dollars to create a place of unceasing worship and prayer right in the heart of the nation's capital? It was both radical and costly and probably seemed absolutely foolish to many people. In the natural there was nothing practical or financially feasible about this model. So, why did he do it? Where did he get the idea? Did David hire 4,288 singers and musicians to sing within earshot of his palace just because he loved music that much? I don't think David's decision was as casual as his love for music or something that he accidentally stumbled upon.

When you take a closer look at David's Tabernacle it's clear that the hand of a master builder was at work. There was great attention given to both detail and design in every component. The other-worldy wisdom displayed in how David structured his kingdom is evidence that he was moved by the spirit of revelation and wisdom. David received nothing less than a divine download, complete with patterns and plans for constructing an exact replica of the Kingdom of Heaven on earth.

When I was a kid my mother was always crafting, baking or sewing something. Those kind of domestic skills just seemed to be the standard for moms of her generation. Making your own clothes was typically a cheaper option so many moms took up this skill as a way to save a few bucks. My mom definitely found ways to live on a limited income, but more than that she just loved to sew. I remember how excited she would get when she found a new pattern for an outfit that caught her eye. As a kid I usually got a front row seat to watch the whole production.

First, she'd unfold a massive cardboard cutting surface and lay it across the bed. By the way, my mom could almost never find her cutting board because I often commandeered it for some new game or fort I was building. Next, she'd pull out a pattern for the dress of her dreams. The pattern was a tissue paper with graphs and lines printed on it, for precision cutting. The pattern usually had very nice images of beautiful models in department-store-quality clothing on the front. The photographs were meant to give the buyer a vision of the stunning outfits they could create with relative ease—if they only followed the pattern.

I watched my mom spend hours, painstakingly cutting and pinning random pieces of fabric to the tissue paper patterns. In the end she'd have dozens of small pieces of fabric laid across the bed ready to be sewn. After a few hours of the chug and grind of the old singer sewing machine she would pull out a dress that looked pretty close to the picture on the package.

The pattern was the key, it contained precision instructions for creating an exact replica of the original. As we study the Tabernacle of David we see that David received a prophetic pattern for replicating the Kingdom of God on earth. Actually there's very little originality to what David did; he outright copied heaven. The structure, heart and principles of David's Kingdom bear a striking resemblance to the throne room scene in Revelation 4.

A Throne Room Glimpse

We have the incredible privilege of having a written record of the sights and sounds of the governmental center of the universe—the very throne room of God. Revelation 4 is a historic, documented, firsthand eyewitness of that invisible realm. This is an insider's look at how God does government. The throne room is the control center of the Kingdom of God, if you will. Before John saw the throne room, David saw it. What John describes in Revelation 4 is almost a mirror image of what King David built on Mt. Zion. Let's take a closer look.

When John entered the door standing open in heaven he was thrust into a mystical swirl of sights and sounds. Heaven is an explosion of color, movement, and songs. Emerald rainbows, flashes of lightning and the "sound of many waters" roar as heaven's citizens release new songs to the Lamb of God! Everything is moving, vibrating and responding to the glory of the "One who is and was and is to come" (Revelation 1:8). All eyes are on Him, gazing on Him, adoring Him, and singing to Him. He is the holy fascination of heaven, and praise is the eternal occupation of all who live there.

His beauty and love are the fuel for sounds and songs that literally never end. His authority is honored night and day as "the twenty-four elders fall down before Him who sits on the throne and worship Him who lives forever and ever, and cast their crowns before the throne..." (Revelation 4:10–11). The simple—but profound—reality of this scene is the King is at the center!

The Center

The Kingdom of heaven revolves around God! He is at the center of it all—this is the primary revelation of the Kingdom of Heaven. If God isn't at the center then it ceases to be the Kingdom of God and becomes the kingdom of men. David came into power in a generation that had rejected the reign of God in favor of a human king. He saw firsthand that when man rules independently of God then fear, control and abuse are the order of the day.

David understood that God resists the proud, but draws near to the humble. He knew that God will not rule, reign and manifest His power where His authority is not honored above all. To David there was no other logical response than to cast his crown before the King of all Kings and to take his place as God's servant. It makes sense then that David put the presence of God right at the center of all of life and culture. He placed the Ark right next to His palace, right in the governmental center of the nation and summoned the nation to honor God night and day.

The songs and prayers going up on the Hill of the Lord rang out over the land as a continual reminder of who they served. The sound of His name could be heard night and day as they lived life and conducted the affairs of the nation. This was an extravagant demonstration of humility and dependence on God to both lead and guide them. As God was given His rightful place as King over the nation, Israel became God's kingdom on earth.

Much of our modern worship and way of doing church has subtly shifted from a God-centered approach to a man-centered one. We have to decide if our primary agenda is to get more people in the church or more of His presence. Whatever we decide will determine our mode of operation. If people are our focus then we will spend a good part of our energy and finances to constantly find bigger and better ways to lure the crowds! Jesus never sought the crowds and yet He was always surrounded by them. As He pursued the Father, the hungry pursued Him.

I think in many ways we've tried to give people what we think they want or need instead of what their hearts are really crying out for. We've spent billions catering to the styles, tastes and needs and all in the name of being relevant. The reality is that very few of us will ever have enough talent and money to compete with the world. If we try to compete with the culture on their playing field we will always lose. We have to remember that the church is a countercultural movement and we possess what every human heart is longing for—His presence. People can pay twenty bucks to get entertained, but they come to church for an encounter with the Divine. If non-believers come to our churches, it's because they are desperate for change, for something real, to experience true love! It's not to say that we shouldn't leverage every available tool to connect to the culture, but if we do this at the expense of the pursuit of His presence, we will lose!

Man-centered methods are leaky wineskins that cannot hold the outpouring of the Holy Spirit. God will not inhabit any model of church that doesn't make His name, word and presence the center of it all. The Tabernacle of David is a reformation of the highest kind: It's a reformation of His presence. David compels us to get God in our midst at all cost! Methods and models that both honor God's presence and provoke the lost to salvation will burst forth from a company of people that have made the pursuit of God the primary activity!

This company of love-sick worshippers will break the molds of dead religion and create containers and spaces that attract God. I've seen God do more through a lone guitarist playing three rusty chords than with a stage full of musicians who have talent and stage presence, but no heart for God. This is exactly what fueled King David to create a place of perpetual honor for the King of all Kings. We would be wise to do the same thing! Let's take a closer look at how David replicated the throne room on Mt. Zion.

Worship in Heaven

The four living creatures, each having six wings, were full of eyes around and within. And they do not rest day or night, saying: "Holy, holy, holy, Lord God Almighty, Who was and is and is to come!"

Whenever the living creatures give glory and honor and thanks to Him who sits on the throne, who lives forever and ever, the twenty-four elders fall down before Him who sits on the throne and worship Him who lives forever and ever, and cast their crowns before the throne, saying:

"You are worthy, O Lord, to receive glory and honor and power; for You created all things, and by Your will they exist and were created" (Revelation 4:8–11).

This is worship in heaven! It is glorious, mysterious and awe-inspiring—and maybe slightly weird.

The Four Chief Worship Leaders in Heaven

In heaven, the chief worship leaders are "the four living creatures, each having six wings, full of eyes around and within" (Revelation 4:8). The prophet Isaiah calls them Seraphim

(Isaiah 6:2), which literally means "burning ones". Their eternal occupation is to "never rest night or day, saying holy, holy, holy…" (Revelation 4:8). Did you ever stop to ask, why do they have eyes all over their body? What purpose did they serve? God made every creature with the necessary equipment to fulfill the purpose they were given. Fish were created with gills so they can live and breathe underwater. Lions are carnivores and so God created them with enough strength, speed and ferocity to live off what they hunt. The seraphim were created to lead worship eternally in heaven, so they were given eyes all around.

That may sound strange, but let me explain. Worship starts with the gift of sight. When we see the beauty, glory and majesty of the eternal God, it awakens worship. The more we see, the more we worship. The Holy Spirit gives us the ability to see, know and experience the invisible God! However, in heaven, God is completely visible and unveiled before all. The seraphim have the high honor of continuously hovering before the open flame of the majesty and glory of the uncreated God. It makes sense that they are called the "burning ones"!

They have been created with multiple eyes which expand their vision to see from multiple angles. They have been endowed with an increased visual capacity to take in more of the incomprehensible beauty and and awe of God. Their expanded view of God is the fuel for their eternal praise. Can you imagine this scene? They continuously fly towards the glory of God to behold Him and then come back to declare to the host of heaven, "Holy, Holy, Holy, Lord God Almighty!" Their praise causes a spontaneous chain reaction of praise among the host of heaven and "the twenty-four elders fall down before Him who sits on the throne and worship" (Revelation 4:9–10).

I love this interchange. I can only imagine the spontaneous outbreaks of worship that go on for thousands of years because of revelatory cries of the Burning Ones. Praise begets praise. Worship from a heart set on fire by the gift of revelation will provoke others to do the same. Do you want to become a better worship leader? The seraphim have the key: Stare at His glorious, awesome beauty until you can't contain it any more! You don't need better techniques for audience participation; you need a fresh glimpse of His glory!

David's Four Burning Ones

Again, David modeled on earth what was in heaven. The seraphim, all with the gift of expanded sight, are the four primary worship leaders in heaven. There were also four worship leaders over the Tabernacle of David. David was the chief worship leader, along with Heman, Jeduthan, and Asaph. These, like David were all prophets and musicians whose primary occupation was "for the ministry of prophesying, accompanied by harps, lyres and cymbals" (1 Chronicles 25:1).

Why did David appoint prophets as the chief worship leaders in Israel? For the same reason the seraphim were appointed as the worship leaders in heaven—they had the gift of sight! The primary purpose of prophecy is to reveal the glory of God to the human heart. God wants us to see and know Him! This isn't an intellectual pursuit but a spiritual one. We cannot see or know Him by mere observation. We are dependent upon the Holy Spirit to open our spiritual eyes. It is these glimpses of His divine nature that provoke us to praise!

Just as the seraphim beheld the glory of the uncreated God and declared His praises, so David and the three prophets positioned themselves to see Him and to sing over the land. Their prophetic songs fueled a nonstop worship movement in Israel for over thirty years! Did they ever dream that God would give them revelation so deep and music so powerful that it would live thousands of years beyond their age and provoke millions to seek the face of God? The songs from this little tent on Mt. Zion have catalyzed revivals, transformed hearts and inspired billions to pursue God! Songs written for the pleasure of man have a short shelf life, but those born in the fires of revelation will live for eternity!

The Twenty-Four Singing Elders

Beside the four living creatures the next level of leadership in heaven are the twenty-four elders. "Around the throne were twenty-four thrones, and on the thrones I saw twenty-four elders, sitting clothed in white, and they had crowns of gold on their head" (Revelation 4:4). Who were the twenty-four elders? They were the highest delegated human authority in the Kingdom of heaven, beside Jesus. Most likely, they were the representatives of both the twelve tribes of Israel and the twelve apostles of Jesus.

What was their job? John further describes them once again in Revelation 5:8, "the twenty-four elders fell down before the Lamb, each having a harp, and golden bowls full of incense, which are the prayers of the saints." Think about it, they were the highest delegated human authority in the universe and their primary and eternal occupation was worship and intercession. Heaven teaches us that authority is released from the place of adoration and intercession. God makes decisions, exacts justice and releases the fullness of His will in the atmosphere of nonstop worship.

The parallels between the structure of David's Tabernacle in 1 Chronicles 25:8–31 with the heavenly order as described in Rev. 4 and 5 are stunning. The first time I read 1 Chronicles 25, I got lost in the long lists of names and frankly got bored and skipped over it. Here's a selection just to give you an idea. This is basically a list of how the 288 appointed singers were grouped:

So the number of them, with their brethren who were instructed in the songs of the Lord, all who were skillful, was two hundred and eighty-eight. And they cast lots for their duty, the small as well as the great, the teacher with the student. Now the first lot for Asaph came out for Joseph; the second for Gedaliah, him with his brethren and sons, twelve; the third for Zaccur, his sons and his brethren, twelve... (1 Chronicles 25:7–9).

Everytime I read this, I missed the revelation hidden between the endless list of names. Then one day, I read it again and by the end of the chapter the light bulb came on! Could it be? Was it here all the time? I painstakingly recounted all the groups of twelve and you guessed it; there were twenty-four twelve-member worship teams all being led by a father or elder. David was undeniably following this heavenly pattern when he chose twenty-four elders to lead unending songs and intercession to the King on Zion.

As David's twenty-four elders gathered their sons together to sing to the Lord night and day, they were, in essence, convening the court of heaven on earth. As they created a place for him on earth that looked like heaven, He bent his ear low and heard their cry and responded with speedy justice. Not only did David hire twenty-four elders to lead 288 singers in worship before the Ark just as in heaven, but he also literally modeled the unceasing nature of prayer in heaven.

24-7 Worship in Heaven

When I was eight years old I remember having a crisis of heart when a friend told me that Heaven would be like one non stop boring church service. I remember thinking, "So, we are just going to sit around singing songs and listening to dull sermons, forever?" I was seriously discouraged at this thought.

Worship never stops in heaven; it goes on night and day, but the reality is we will never be bored! It's our destiny to be eternally fascinated by the glory and beauty of the God. The living creatures, elders, angels and the host of heaven have one holy occupation: to adore the King. Revelation 4:8 tells us they "do not rest day or night saying 'holy, holy, holy is the Lord God almighty, who is and was and is to come." Worship never ends because His worth never ends! He is worthy of unceasing, eternal praise! This alone is enough reason to devote the entirety of our lives and exhaust all of our resources to give Him unceasing praise.

24-7 Worship in David's Tent

Once again, David copied heaven. He pioneered the first recorded account of perpetual musical worship and prayer in the earth. 1 Chronicles says that David "left there before the ark of the covenant of the LORD Asaph and his brethren, to minister before the ark continually, as every day's work required" (16:37). Establishing twenty-four elders to lead worship was not only revelatory, but it was very practical. Having twenty-four meant that they could assign a team to sing in succession every hour of the day.

He gave 4,288 singers and musicians full-time jobs to minister to the Lord (1 Chronicles 9:33), to prophesy on their instruments (1 Chronicles 25:1) and to pray the prayers of heaven. On top of that, there were another 4,000 gatekeepers who attended to all the daily needs of operating a night and day worship ministry for the multitudes. Several thousand people were employed in the service of worship. By today's standards that meant David spent about $30 million per month to steward night and day worship. For thirty-three years the love song to Yahweh never ended and the results were astounding!

Think about it: David gave his people the gift of a perpetual open heaven. An entire generation grew up dreaming, working, living, and building the Kingdom of God on earth in this presence soaked atmosphere. As they gave the King of Glory His rightful place of authority over the land, God gave them authority over the nations.

David modeled heaven on earth when he set up his tabernacle of worship. He built a copy of the Kingdom of God on earth. Let's review what he did:

Throne Room Worship

- God, the King is at the center of all activity and worship in heaven (Revelation 4)

- Four living creatures with the gift of sight, lead perpetual worship in heaven (Revelation 4)

- Twenty-four elders worship night and day in heaven (Revelation 4)

- Perpetual worship in Heaven

David's Tabernacle

- David crowned God King and made worship the central feature of his government

- Four prophets led worship in Israel, David, Heman, Jeduthan, Asaph (1 Chronicles 25:1)

- Twenty-four elders lead twenty-four worship teams on earth (1 Chronicles 25)

- Perpetual worship on earth

David built nothing less than a beautiful replica of the throne of God in the earth. But why? Why does God want copies of the throne room on earth? What purpose does it serve?

Moses' Tabernacle was also " a copy and shadow of the heavenly things" (Hebrews 8:5). It's easy to get lost in the intricate details of Moses' Tabernacle and the layers and layers of protocol given for proper worship and sacrifices and totally miss the heartbeat of why God wanted him to build it. God asked them to "... make Me a sanctuary, that I may dwell among them" (Exodus 25:8). God's burning desire from the beginning of all time was to live and dwell on earth with man! This is the first and most important reason that God wanted copies of heaven on earth! It was partially realized in both Moses' and David's tabernacle and fully realized in Jesus.

Secondly, God wanted to dwell on earth with men in order to expand the borders of His kingdom on earth. As we model on earth what's going on in heaven, He brings heaven to earth. God rules from the place of praise and prayer. We literally convene the government of God in the earth as we worship. As we cry out to God, He releases justice in the earth, pushes back the works of darkness and expands His Kingdom on earth!

Don't despise your small prayer gatherings. Numbers are not significant in the Kingdom of God. Every major revival has its origins with a small band of intercessors faithfully crying out! Small gatherings precede big breakthroughs! When we gather to worship and pray, regardless of size, we convene the very court of heaven on earth. Our prayer gatherings are the most important and powerful meetings in our city. The prayer room is where the fate and destiny of our city is decided!

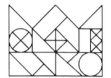

Was David's Tabernacle 24-7?

When I got involved in the prayer movement I heard many passionate sermons and teachings declaring that David's Tabernacle was a literal twenty-four hour, seven days a week reality. Honestly, I heard it so much and from so many reputable teachers that I never even questioned it—probably not the smartest move on my part. I read a lot of books, attended several conferences and not one person ever gave scriptural references to prove or disprove this idea. It seemed like this was the general consensus and basic assumption from most people I talked to in the prayer movement. I thought, "There's gotta be something everyone knows that I don't."

So, I began the journey of studying this topic for myself. As I studied, I was frustrated that I couldn't find any verses that explicitly stated that David's Tabernacle implemented twenty-four hour worship and prayer. I kept thinking, "I must not know how to find these mysterious references." Eventually, I came across several verses that alluded to the idea, but I always felt most people stretched these to make them fit.

Several years later I had the honor of driving a prominent leader of the prayer movement back and forth from his hotel for the conference he was speaking at. After several minutes of great conversation, I finally mustered the courage to ask him if he thought there was enough Biblical evidence to support the idea that David's Tabernacle was literally 24-7. I was secretly hoping he had conclusive evidence that the Tabernacle of David was in fact, 24-7. To my disappointment, he made the honest and humble confession that he didn't believe there was enough explicit Biblical proof to confirm that worship in David's time was nonstop.

Well, there you go, case closed, or so I thought. A few weeks later I had a sudden moment of enlightenment when I was preparing to do a question and answer session on the Tabernacle of David for the Burn 24-7 online school called Field Training. It was like finding a missing piece to a puzzle. What I discovered tipped me over the edge in my thinking. I'd like to share with you what I discovered and why I now believe that the weight of evidence supports the idea that David led Israel into night and day worship and prayer. But ultimately, you can decide.

David Inherited a 24–7 Model

Leviticus 6:13, says, "A fire shall always be burning on the altar; it shall never go out." This is one of the most popular verses used in the 24-7 prayer movement. It's one of those verses that really looks good on prayer room walls, t-shirts or on websites, but is often misused and taken out of context. When I read this verse I was immediately inspired to find out what it really meant. Was this verse being used out of context? Did it have any connection to worship and prayer or was it just a nice cliché for the house of prayer? I was absolutely shocked at what I discovered.

If you back up to Leviticus 6:9, it says "...the burnt offering shall be on the hearth upon the altar all night until morning, and the fire of the altar shall be kept burning on it." It took me a couple of minutes of reading this passage before the lights came on. I read and reread it and finally I saw it. There it was! It wasn't hidden at all. It was plain for all to see. "...the fire shall be kept on the altar all night until morning..." Did this say what I think it did? Could Moses' Tabernacle also have been a 24-7 reality?

Think about it, the instructions were to keep the fire burning all night. Can you imagine the volume of work that went into this job? Someone had to chop the wood, haul it to the tabernacle, add it the fire, remove the ashes and keep the flames stoked. The next day the work didn't stop and the fire kept burning as they were instructed to offer both a morning and evening sacrifice. What happened between these two sacrifices? The fires were kept burning as worshippers would present their offerings before the Lord all day long. This fire literally burned twenty-four hours a day.

Practically speaking there wasn't a need to tend a fire during the night watches. Everyone was sleeping, no one was bringing sacrifices to burn at two o'clock in the morning. So, why did they do it? The Altar wasn't just a place of sacrifice, but a place of prayer also. Priests kept watch all night so that the altar of devotion and prayer would never cease in Israel. Could it be that this perpetual flame was meant to replicate the unceasing fire of worship that burned before the Lord in heaven?

Hebrews 8:5 tells us that the Tabernacle of Moses was to be " a copy and shadow of the heavenly things." Every component of this earthly tabernacle represented a heavenly reality. Worship never stops in heaven, so it makes sense that it would never stop in Moses' Tabernacle.

Moses' Tabernacle was the only frame of reference that King David had for worship. It's where he got his theology and drew his inspiration. David built upon and expanded this legacy of worship by including musical worship. Animal sacrifice didn't cease in David's day, but he introduced a new kind of sacrifice, the sacrifice of praise.

Continually Means Continually

When David set up his worship tabernacle, "he left there before the ark of the covenant of the LORD Asaph and his brethren, to minister before the ark continually, as every day's work required" (1 Chronicles 16:37 KJV). I looked up the Hebrew word for *continually* and I was surprised to find that it means what it says: continually. It also means perpetual, always, and evermore. The next part of the verse says, "as each day's work required." What were the daily duties of the priests? As we saw in the last point, the priestly duties included offering both a morning and evening sacrifice, all the sacrifices in between and tending the fire on the Altar through the night watch.

In this case, David added singers and musicians to minister to the Lord, alongside the regular sacrifices. Can you imagine what it was like to sing to the Lord about His mercy and forgiveness, while animals were being slaughtered for your redemption right in front of your eyes? Could it be that the great prophetic songs about Jesus, the sacrificial Lamb of God were sung during these moments?

The Structure Supports It

In 1 Chronicles 25, David describes the structure of singers in the Tabernacle. He could have set this up anyway he wanted, yet he appointed twenty-four elders to lead twenty-four twelve-member worship teams. As previously discussed, the twenty-four elders mirrored the twenty-four elders who worship night and day in heaven. I believe this structure was as practical as it was spiritual. Having twenty-four teams gave them the ability to divide the workload to keep the fires of worship burning twenty-four hours a day.

The Volume of People He Employed

"Those who were musicians, heads of Levite families, stayed in the rooms of the temple and were exempt from other duties because they were responsible for the work day and night" (1 Chronicles 9:33 NIV).

"Moreover he commanded the people who dwelt in Jerusalem to contribute support for the priests and the Levites, that they might devote themselves to the Law of the Lord" (2 Chronicles 31:4 NASB).

Why would he need to hire 288 singers and 4,000 musicians if he didn't have work for them? These were not bi-vocational musicians, they were "exempt from other duties", meaning they were full-time singers. It goes on to explain that the reason they were exempt from other duties was "because they were responsible for the work day and night." Think about it, a twenty-four hour place of worship would require a massive workforce so David was merely staffing according to the needs.

He spared no expense to host God's presence. He spent the equivalent of $30 million a month to employ thousands of people in worship to the King. For the first time in Israel's history, singers and musicians were given full-time jobs to sing to the Lord night and day.

Not the Model but the Heart

So, what's the bottom line? Does this mean that we need to abandon all pursuits and build twenty-four-hour houses of prayer? For those called to this, I say, yes! David's Tabernacle is a wineskin for radical devotion to God. It gives a context for those called to be vocational worshippers or intercessors to fulfill their calling. God is raising up houses of prayer all over the earth inspired by the Davidic model. But, not all are called to do this. We cannot look at David's Tabernacle as another method to be followed.

God isn't looking for us to follow some legalistic model or standard of ministry. If we get caught up in the structure we will completely miss the point. The very core of David's tabernacle is about intimacy and partnership with God. David's tabernacle calls us back to our priestly calling to live and enjoy God's presence as well as our kingly call to take dominion over the earth. The heart and principles of David's Tabernacle are what is being restored. Even if you can shoot holes in all my theories about the Tabernacle of David being a literal place 24-7 worship, you can't argue that He is worthy of night and day worship and prayer! We will never exhaust the glory and wealth of the King of all kings!

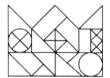

Chapter 6

THE KINGDOM THREAD

If your take a carburetor out of a car engine and study it, you can learn a lot of interesting things. However, you can't really know everything about this part until you understand how it fits in and relates to the rest of the engine. By itself, a carburetor is useless, but when it is fully functional and connected to the whole engine it's actually inexpendable. I find that most studies on worship and prayer are like this. We treat them as isolated topics and forget that they are connected to a bigger picture—the Kingdom of God. When you see the role of worship and prayer in the Kingdom of God, you see how inseparable they are to God's masterplan.

David's tabernacle wasn't a worship and prayer movement, it was a Kingdom movement. David built an earthly kingdom after the pattern of heaven. His model gives us a clear example of what the Kingdom of God is like and how God partners with man to extend its borders. The principles and patterns of the Tabernacle of David serve as a blueprint for all generations for releasing the reign of God in the earth.

The First Kingdom

What David did was revolutionary, but it wasn't new. He tapped into the ancient foundations of the Kingdom of God that finds its roots in the Garden of Eden. Eden was the very first expression of the Kingdom of God on earth. The first three chapters of Genesis are a pure, undefiled peek into what God always intended when He created the heavens and the earth. These chapters are a historic glimpse into planet earth when it was brand new and everything was functioning according to God's intended purpose. The revelation packed into these few verses are the foundation and heartbeat of humanity; they are God's highest ideal.

In Genesis we see the transcendent, uncreated, all powerful God walking in the cool of the day with children (Genesis 3:8). He's not floating on a cloud of superiority or peering over the balcony of heaven, aloof and unavailable in all of His holiness and splendor. But, rather, we find His feet right in the dirt with those He created. The Garden was the place where heaven merged with earth—God with man, no separation.

Think about it. Adam and Eve lived, worked, played and created in the continual atmosphere of God's glorious, and life-giving presence. His presence was their perfect home and their native habitat. In the realm of perfect love, absent of all fear, mankind was absolutely free to soar to the heights of their God given potential. Eden was the model for what life was meant to be; it was God's Kingdom on earth. It's a picture of our original design and our destiny. Eden preaches to us the glorious gospel: "God loves you and want to be with you! Your home is His presence, your destiny is to live life from this place."

Our First Calling—Communion

In Eden, we see that the first and primary calling of humanity is to live in communion and fellowship with God. This speaks of our priestly calling before the Lord. I'm not speaking about our modern understanding of the priesthood with robes and collars. The priests were those called out, consecrated and given access to very presence of God. This was the destiny of all mankind, not just a select few.

The greatest tragedy of all time was when Adam and Eve sinned and were banished from His presence. They fell from their highest calling to be priests unto the Lord. This grieved God's heart more than anything. From that moment on His children began to wither and die like a beautiful flower plucked from the soil. Humanity couldn't survive outside of the air of His life-giving presence. In the darkness man was vulnerable to the lies of fear and shame. Sin ate away at the soul of man like a disease and distorted and perverted God's original design. Thus began the greatest pursuit of all time!

The whole point of the gospel was to give man access back to the presence of God! This is why He paid the highest price, by giving the very life of His son on the cross. This is the divine romance and the most extravagant love story in history. Love is God's core value and the motivation behind everything He does. It was the primary reason God asked men to build replicas of His throne on earth. He was basically telling them, "If you build it, I will come" and come He did. He manifested His glorious presence in the holy of holies and in partial measure gave man back their destiny to live life in His presence.

David's Tabernacle was nothing less than a glorious revival of God's original intentions for mankind. David built His kingdom on the revelation that God longs to be with those He created. In David's tabernacle we see that intimacy with God is written into our very DNA and that the primary identity of man is to be a priest unto God. David restored his entire generation back to their calling to be a kingdom of priests (Exodus 19:6, Revelation 1:6).

Our Second Calling—Dominion

Adam and Eve were the picture of everything man was meant to be. They were not only priests, but kings also. Revelation 1:6 says, "...and (He has) made us **kings** and priests to His God and Father, to Him be glory and dominion forever and ever. Amen." (emphasis mine). These are the two core identities and callings of every believer. Their priestly calling was to live in constant communion with God, but their kingly calling was to partner with God to expand the borders of Eden across the earth.

Did you know God created you to be His partner in ruling over creation? Everything that God created was designed with our participation in mind. The earth could not come into its full potential without the partnership of man. Most of what God created was in seed form. God provided the seed, the soil, and the rain, but for the land to reach its highest purpose for food, pleasure and beauty, it needed a man to cultivate the ground. When God created the earth He left much of it unformed and thereby placed a demand on His sons and daughters to use their vision, creativity and labor to make it into something beautiful. God has given us seeds full of promise, which can only be released by those with the passion and determination to make them into a garden of delight. Our mandate as sons of God is to work with God to bring the fullness of His dream for every man to pass.

To explore, conquer, lead, achieve, win and triumph to some degree or another beats in the heart of every man. Dominion was written into the fabric of man's soul at the beginning. God gave man the mandate to subdue the earth and to take dominion over every living thing (Genesis 1:28). Human beings were not created to be a slave class that merely carried out God's wishes. We were actually given the highest position of authority in the earth. Our job is to steward, subdue and rule over all of God's creation. This is God's chosen authority structure, and He's committed to it. He won't override the power and authority He gave us. God gave us free will, which is another indicator of our calling to reign. God gives us the freedom to choose what we want and ultimately decide our destiny. This is a sobering thought and high calling.

Dominion Lost

Just outside the borders of the beautiful and lush garden home was a wild and uninhabitable domain that could only be transformed through the love, creativity and hard work of man. The ultimate vision was for Adam and Eve to live, work and lead their families right in the center of His presence. The idea was for them to grow their family and for each member to use their unique talents and abilities to build cities around the presence of God.

As they stayed loyal to their friendship and devotion to God they would always stand in their delegated sphere of authority as kings over the earth. When man was created, Satan was present.

Satan was cast down from heaven because he exalted himself above the glory of God. Heaven's orphan son then roamed through the earth, hungry for worship, thirsting for power and looking for a kingdom to rule. The creation of man was Satan's greatest threat, for they were created in the image and likeness of God. God's solution to deal with the presence of evil in the earth was to create beings in His own likeness and give the dominion and leadership over all living things, including Satan.

There was only one rule in the garden: do not eat from the tree of knowledge of good and evil. God gave man a choice in order to daily exercise both their freedom and love for God through their obedience. Without a choice man could never fully express their identity to be kings and rulers of the earth. By staying in agreement with His will, God's children would displace the powers of darkness. The only way for Satan to rule is for us to give him our place. He is constantly looking for ways to get us to concede our position of authority over the earth.

By listening to Satan, Adam gave the enemy a place of authority over the earth that he never should have had. This was the tragic moment when we went from reigning kings to suffering slaves. The only way Satan can have any influence in the earth is when we, as God's representative authority, make agreements with him. The decisions we make either open or shut doors for evil or righteousness to rule over the earth. What we agree with, we empower.

The Power of Agreement

One time I was leading worship at about 2:00 a.m. at our local Prayer Furnace in Shawnee, Oklahoma and I heard this phrase in my spirit, "Agreement is the place where heaven meets earth!" Immediately my spirit surged with this revelation and I began to sing and shout it. It's the simple reality that when we agree with God's Word we give God a place to enforce it in the earth. Our agreement opens the door for His realm to influence ours. Why does God want our agreement?

We are God's representative authority in the earth and He will not cross our free will. He has actually given stewardship and dominion over the earth realm to us. This is a very sobering thought. If we don't want God to come, He won't. If we don't want His Word, His will, His presence, we don't have to have it. Saul's generation didn't want God to be King, so He gave them a man to rule over them. He will let us have what we want.

So, we as rulers over the earth, hold incredible sway over what happens here. When we honor God's authority and agree with His Word, we actually release Him to rule over the earth. This is exactly why David built a governmental structure that was fueled by night and day worship and prayer. David had the revelation that God "is enthroned on the praises of His people" (Psalm 22:3 NLT).

In other words, God will set His throne among and rule from praise, just as in heaven. David understood the principle of agreement. He knew the authority that mankind wielded in the earth. He saw the abuse of this power in Saul, who opened the floodgates of rebellion and evil over Israel. When David came into power, he slammed the doors shut that Saul had opened and then set up a center of perpetual agreement with the King of Glory. Every single activity of David's Tabernacle was a form of agreement with God. Let's take a look at these activities:

1. **Praise, Agreement with God's Nature**. Praise simply means to honor who He is, and what He's like. Through perpetual praise they both welcomed and gave God His rightful place of authority in the land. As they sang about His nature, He manifested and revealed Himself to them. Some of the most profound songs and poems about the nature of God were penned and sung in David's Tabernacle.

2. **Thanksgiving, Agreement with What He Has Done**. There were actually those in David's Tabernacle that had the full-time job of thanking God. Why? Thanksgiving is powerful. Thanksgiving is a call to re-member the testimonies of God's faithfulness, love and mercy. As we thank God for what He did, it stirs hope and faith for what He is going to do. Thanksgiving causes faith to stay at high octane and our trust in God to remain firm. The very reason that Israel abandoned God

in David's early days is because they forgot. Thanksgiving releases bursts of joy as we remember all that God has done. The "thankers" must have been the happiest people in Israel. I'm sure you could always spot the "thankers" who were laughing and dancing continually in the house of God. Their full-time occupation was to remind the nation of the goodness of God. They were poets of hope

3. **Intercession, Agreement with His Will.** Intercession is a form of agreement with God's will. What is God's will? God's will is for all humanity to be restored back to their original design. Agreeing that God's will empowers God to release the resources of heaven into the earth.

4. **Prophetic: Agreement with What He's Going to Do.** Through the gift of prophecy we have the ability to see the incredible things God has prepared for us. When we prophesy we are agreeing with what God wants to do; we keep our hearts aligned with and anchored in hope.

These are the perpetual activities of the throne room of God. It's how God does government. God has chosen to rule in and through unceasing night and day praise, thanksgiving, intercession and the prophetic. As God's chosen authority in the earth it's only when we come into full agreement with His nature and will that His kingdom will be extended in the earth. As David modeled on Zion what was going on in heaven, he built a throne for God to rule over His creation.

The message of David's Tabernacle screams, "Build it and they will come!" As we build places of honor and agreement with the King of Glory, He will surely come. The Kingdom expands and influences nations at the sound of His bride singing, declaring and praying His heart. The foundation of His throne on earth is built in the hearts of worshipers who have cast their crowns down before Him.

Chapter 7

SNEAK PREVIEW

"Oh man, that looks awesome! That's going to be the coolest movie ever... I'm totally going to see that!" I often overhear comments like this while sitting through the previews at the movies. I love movie trailers, sometimes more than the actual movie itself. The trailer isn't the whole movie, it's just a taste. These short, fast-moving clips are meant to wow you, incite your curiosity and ultimately get you to go see it.

What David did, how he built his kingdom was profound in and of itself, but it was just a sneak preview—the trailer for the greatest human drama planet earth has ever seen. The Tabernacle of David was one massive prophetic word that pointed to Jesus. Let's look at what David did.

"Who may ascend into hill of the Lord?" (Psalm 24:3). This is the question David asked the brave pioneers who gathered to bring the Ark up to Mt. Zion. The memories of the tragic death of their friend and brother Uzzah would have been fresh in their minds (2 Samuel 6:7). They must have been asking themselves, "Am I qualified? Will I make it up Mt. Zion without dying?" Those who joined David on the second attempt must have either been totally crazy or consumed with the vision for hosting God's presence in the earth. What David was asking them to do was absolutely life threatening and broke hundreds of years of protocol under the Mosaic tradition.

River of Blood

David wanted to make sure that every heart was prepared to stand before the Ark of His presence on Mt. Zion. So they sacrificed oxen and sheep every six steps all the way up the Mountain (2 Samuel 6:13). Think about the reality of this! This must have been an incredibly noisy and bloody scene. As they slaughtered hundreds of animals, a river of blood ran down the mountain and stained the feet of the worshipers as they carried the Ark up to Mt. Zion. Can you imagine the soberness and spirit of repentance as they passed lamb after lamb, which had been slaughtered in order to cover their sins? This was a powerful prophetic picture of Jesus who would march up Golgotha's hill and shed His blood to reconcile man back to God.

Unveiled Worship

In Moses' Tabernacle, the Ark was to remain behind a veil in the holy of holies and only one priest could approach the throne of God. Yet David did something unheard of and absolutely revolutionary. He placed the Ark under a tent, with no veil, giving everyone access to worship God on the mountain night and day (2 Samuel 6:1–19). Moses' Tabernacle and the sacrificial system of worship continued on Mt. Gibeon (1 Chronicles 16:39), but the holy of holies was moved to Mt. Zion.

It may have looked like David broke the law or even disregarded God's original intentions for worship when he did this, but this was anything but rebellion. David was compelled by the Spirit of the Lord to give the earth a preview of what was coming when the Messiah would rip the veil and give humanity access to God's presence again (Matthew 27:51). Access to God! This was the point of it all. God wanted to restore man back to the place intimate union with Himself. He paid the ultimate price in sending His son and all for this one reason.

Thirty-Three Years

David's generation was given the unique grace to live a New Testament reality in the Old Testament. Even the number of years that David hosted unveiled worship, pointed to Jesus. From the moment he brought up the Ark to Mt. Zion until his death was a total of thirty-three years (2 Samuel 5:5). This was the exact number of years that Christ lived on earth. Israel lived out a prophetic word that pointed to the God-man, Jesus Christ, who would take the sins of mankind upon himself and give humanity unrestricted access to the presence of God.

The Eternal Throne

God spoke to David quite a lot about the coming Messiah. The Psalms have documented several prophetic songs about Jesus that were sung at least 1,000 years before He came. God honored David at the end of his life and gave him a stunning prophetic promise: "Your house and your kingdom shall be established forever before you. Your throne shall be established forever" (2 Samuel 7:16). He used the word "forever" which means even beyond this life David would have a son sit on the throne. This undeniably pointed to Jesus. The New Testament boldly declares that Jesus is the promised son of David that will reign eternally on his throne:

- "The book of the genealogy of Jesus Christ, the Son of David, the Son of Abraham" (Matthew 1:1).

- "He will be great, and will be called the Son of the Highest; and the Lord God will give Him the throne of His father David. And He will reign over the house of Jacob forever, and of His kingdom there will be no end" (Luke 1:32–33).

- All the crowds were amazed, and were saying, "This man cannot be the Son of David, can he?" (Matthew 12:23).

I wonder if David ever dreamt that God Himself would come in the flesh, be born into his royal line and sit on the throne eternally? What David did was absolutely revolutionary! It became a holy example to all generations for how the Kingdom of God is established on earth. His Kingdom is a perfect picture of what God always intended. As glorious as all this was, it was but a mere shadow in comparison to the glory of the Kingdom to come with Jesus. Jesus, is the ultimate fulfillment of the

Tabernacle of David! What David did in part, Jesus did in the fullness.

The Kingdom is at Hand

When Jesus came began His ministry, He came proclaiming that the Kingdom of God was at hand (Matthew 4:17). He came to take His rightful place as the heir to David's Throne. Those in His day would have expected the Messiah to be a military leader who would take an actual, earthly position of leadership over the nation. However, Jesus didn't come to restore a geo-political empire; He came to bring the very Kingdom of God to earth. This was a Kingdom that would find its full expression in the hearts of men. This was a radical concept and even though it was right in front of their faces most people couldn't perceive it.

Jesus Restores Order

A few years ago I was leading worship at 3:00 a.m. at an all-night Burn 24-7 event. I love those early morning moments when the only people in the room are those crazy enough and hungry enough to stay up all night. At one point the spirit of prophecy came on me as I was singing my way through Psalm 24. When I came to verse seven it was like electric currents pulsating through my body as I sang "Open up the gates and let the King of Glory come in" (Psalm 24:7)! I must have sang this for over an hour! I could feel the spirit of God pleading with the church of our city to open the doors to His presence. At one point I was literally screaming at the top of my lungs, "Open up the gates!" over and over.

In the middle of shouting like a crazy man, I saw a vision of Jesus riding into Jerusalem. But what I saw shocked me. It wasn't the typical picture of gentle Jesus holding a lamb, patting children on the head and smiling. What I saw was a King with a look of fury on his face. He rode into Jerusalem with fire in His eyes and a whip in his hands. As He approached the temple, He cried out, "My house will be called a house of prayer!" And He turned tables, sending all the money changers running! When the dust settled, God said to me, "Be sure you know who you are inviting into your city! I am the King and I've come to turn the tables of religion and put things in order! I am the King, and there can be no other."

When Jesus came into the world, the kingdom of David was in ruins. There was a famine of true worship in the Israel. Until John the Baptist, there hadn't been a prophetic voice in the land for over 400 years. In the absence of revelation, Israel became a cold, legalistic, loveless and hard hearted people. They excelled at all the outward forms of religion but their hearts were far from God. They were a sick, broken and twisted version of what God intended for His people. The spiritual leaders were self-seeking and full of corruption. They used fear and control to accomplish their ungodly pursuits for power and wealth. When Jesus came, His mission was to bring the superior Kingdom of God to earth. He came with the fiery zeal of reformation to put Israel back on the right foundations. Let's look closer at what Jesus did.

Jesus' First Move

"And the multitudes that went before, and that followed, cried, saying, Hosanna to the Son of David: Blessed is He that cometh in the name of the Lord; Hosanna in the highest" (Matthew 21:9).

When they cried out, "Hosanna to the Son of David", it was a profound and revelatory moment; they saw Jesus for who He was. They honored him as David's son, the promised Messianic King. Their praise built a highway for Jesus as He rode into Jerusalem to take His place. His first act as King was reminiscent of what David did when he took the throne. David's first act was to bring reformation to the place of worship and so it was with Jesus. What did Jesus do first? He went straight to the "temple of God, and cast out all them that sold and bought in the temple, and overthrew the tables of the moneychangers, and the seats of them that sold doves" (Matthew 21:12).

Think about this scene. In the midst of praise, while children were still chanting "Hosanna!" the King of all Kings unleashed the whip of reformation and drove out the mercenaries. He took His place in the midst of praise. He didn't take time to convince them of His authority. He simply took His place. Why did Jesus do this? Jesus knew that to lead and transform the nation, He had to bring reformation to the place of worship first. They were out of order! Worship had become a man centered, greed-fueled enterprise. Jesus confronted the dysfunctional religious system that wasn't fit to host the King of Kings. Why? Because God only reigns where He's honored. If they were to be revived, then the house of the Lord had to return to it's original calling.

Right after Jesus flipped the tables, He proclaimed this message: "My house shall be called the house of prayer; but you have made it a den of thieves" (Matthew 21:13). In this one statement Jesus called the people of God back to their identity to be a house of prayer. This is the foundation of the Kingdom of God! The Kingdom is about the King! It's about the King dwelling with those He made. He's reminding them that they are called to host God's presence in the earth and to create a place of unbroken communion. He tapped into the heart of David who built a government and life built around worship and prayer. The house of prayer is the primary paradigm for how the Kingdom of God expands in the earth.

After Jesus brought divine order back to the house of worship, "the blind and the lame came to him in the temple; and he healed them" (Matthew 21:14). This is such a beautiful picture of how the Kingdom works. Authority and power will emerge from the house of prayer. He will be enthroned in our praises. He will manifest His glory wherever he is honored. We have yet to see the kind of power and miracles that will come as we return to the heart and ways of God!

Jesus Models the Tabernacle of David
The heart and principles of David's Tabernacle are woven through the teaching of Jesus. Worship is the first order of importance when Jesus taught them to pray. Matthew 6:13 tell us, "In this manner, therefore, pray, Our Father in heaven, hallowed by your name." Why is worship the first and highest priority in the Kingdom of God? Because, If God is not at the center then it ceases to be the Kingdom of God, but of man. Continual worship keeps our hearts in alignment with His

Kingship. God always manifests where He is worshipped and honored.

Secondly He tells them to pray, "Your kingdom come. Your will be done on earth as it is in heaven." This is the mission statement of the church. Our job is to bring the superior kingdom of God to the earth and it starts by asking. Jesus teaches that the Kingdom of God advances and is established through the humility of worship and prayer. God will always honor prayers prayed in agreement with His will and purpose!

The Upper Room
We see this same principle throughout the book of Acts. The church was born in the fires of a 10-day prayer meeting leading up to the day of Pentecost (Acts 2). After days of waiting on God, the fire of the Holy Spirit filled them with incredible power and boldness, resulting in thousands coming into the Kingdom. Revival and harvest were the byproducts of hearts that turned to God in worship and prayer.

Antioch
The church of Antioch (Acts 13) was the apostolic center of the emerging Church. Out of the place of continual fasting and prayer God raised up missionaries and sent them to the known world. The harvest will come to the places of prayer. We see this repeated over and over throughout history.

Jesus Restored David's Tabernacle
Jesus is the ultimate fulfillment of the Tabernacle of David. He ripped the veil and restored man back to their priestly calling, to live and commune with the living God. He liberated mankind from the slavery of sin and sickness. He released man from the bondage of Satan's dominion and restored man back to their rightful place as the kings of the earth. Before He ascended to heaven, He commissioned all of humanity to bring the Kingdom of God to earth! He baptized us with the Holy Spirit and authorized us to represent heaven on earth. We are co-laborers with Jesus in this great work of global transformation.

Chapter 8

HUNGER PAINS OF REVIVAL

Never have I heard so many people talk about revival. As I travel across the world I hear dozens of passionate believers say things like, "I'm not sure what's going on, but I just sense we are on the brink of a massive move of God." It's like there is a corporate knowing that an unprecedented revival is on the horizon. I love that many of the prayer groups I encounter are convinced that their city will be the destination of the next big revival.

Historically speaking, revival movements usually happen from a few geographical locations and spread around the world from there. Could it be that all those hearing words about revival coming to their city, are right? Yes! God is speaking and preparing us for an outpouring of the Holy Spirit that will flood the earth like a tidal wave. I believe every place that hungry people call on the name of the Lord will become a landing place for revival.

Have you ever been hungry, I mean, truly hungry? I remember going on a forty-day fast and by day three I was seeing visions of hamburgers and pizza. The physical hunger pains kept my thoughts in an endless loop of dreaming about food and resisting the urge to eat. Hunger compels and drives us to satisfy our appetite. Spiritual hunger is a precedent to all great moves of God.

Prophecy is one of the most important keys to revival because it awakens our spiritual hunger. God has been speaking often and loudly that a wave of revival is coming beyond our wildest imaginations. These prophecies are meant to get our hopes up and cause us to pray, fight and believe until we see them come to pass. Amos 9:11–15 gives us a vivid picture of what we can expect in this last-day outpouring:

> "On that day I will raise up the tabernacle of David, which has fallen down, and repair its damages; I will raise up its ruins, and rebuild it as in the days of old; that they may possess the remnant of Edom, and all the Gentiles who are called by My name," says the Lord who does this thing.

> "Behold, the days are coming," says the Lord, "When the plowman shall overtake the reaper, and the treader of grapes him who sows seed; the mountains shall drip with sweet wine, and all the hills shall flow with it. I will bring back the captives of My people Israel; they shall build the waste cities and inhabit them; they shall plant vineyards and drink wine from them; they shall also make gardens and eat fruit from them. I will plant them in their land, and no longer shall they be pulled up from the land I have given them," says the Lord your God.

First, let's give some context to this prophetic word. Two hundred and fifty years after the fires of revival burned on Mt. Zion, Israel was wayward, cold and sitting in the ash heap of the former move of God. During the days of Amos, Israel was but a shell of their former glory under King David. Amos described them as broken, fallen, ruined and in need of repair (Amos 9:11). From the ruins of the once glorious Davidic Kingdom, Amos prophesied a restoration beyond everyone's wildest imagination. He declared that the fallen Tabernacle of David would be resurrected and usher in the greatest days of revival humanity has ever seen. This prophecy is a picture of our future! As you read let faith arise and hunger be provoked for what God has planned!

Unprecedented Harvest

There are multiplied millions of people that have yet to hear the gospel one time! There are about 9,000 people groups classified as unreached. Pew Research estimates that to be roughly 1.8 billion people; 24% of the population are Muslim. The task of global evangelization is staggering and the needs are overwhelming. The current state of the western church is bleak at best. Thankfully, our hope isn't in man or man made institutions, but in God. As we look at the promises of God in Amos, our hopes can soar! Amos declares nothing less than the greatest harvest of souls in human history! Let's take a look:

"That they may possess the remnant of Edom, and all the Gentiles who are called by My name," says the LORD who does this thing (Vs. 12).

When I read this verse I thought, "Who is Edom? What does it mean that they will possess the remnant of Edom?" The Edomites were the descendants of Esau. Modern day Muslims trace their lineage back to Esau. If you remember the story, there was a bitter division between Jacob and Esau, which caused a generational divide between all their descendants. The original hearers of this prophecy would have probably interpreted this to mean that Israel would possess them in the military sense. However, this wasn't what God had in mind.

The book of Acts gives us a clearer picture of God's intention. The Apostle James quotes Amos 9:11–12 in response to the news that the gospel was spreading like wildfire among the Gentiles. The term *gentile* was a generic term referring to anyone who wasn't a Jew—which, of course, included the Edomites. Gentiles were considered heathen and outside the realm of God's saving grace. For them to receive the gospel would have blown the apostles' theological minds. When James declared this prophecy from Amos it's as if the light bulb was going off, a sudden reality that they were experiencing its fulfillment. In essence, James paraphrased Amos 9:11–12 like this: "After this I will return and will rebuild the tabernacle of David, which has fallen down....so that the rest of humanity may seek the Lord, even the Gentiles who are called by name (Acts 15:16-17).

He replaces the original phrase, "that they may possess the remnant of Edom" with "that all humanity will seek the Lord..." James got it! He saw that possessing Edom wasn't a military maneuver, but a missions movement. He connected the unprecedented wave of Gentiles seeking Christ as a fulfillment of Amos 9:11–12. James had the powerful revelation that Jesus had ripped the door open and made a way for all nations to come to Him. King Jesus didn't come to take dominion over the nations through military might, but through love. He wasn't interested in enslaving the Edomites, but adopting them back into the family. Jesus was God's extravagant offering to the nations. He gave the lost, broken and ruined humanity an open door into His house. The book of Acts was merely the starting gate of this global harvest of souls!

Since those days the gospel has been advancing with a violent force. Today, there are more people who identify themselves as Christians than the total population of planet earth when the book of Acts was written. What both Amos and James declared is that restoration of the Tabernacle of David will lead the greatest harvest of souls humanity has ever seen.

An Accelerated Harvest of Souls
"Behold the days are coming says the Lord, when the plowman shall overtake the reaper and the treader of grapes him who sows seed" (Acts 9:13).

Amos uses a powerful metaphor to help us see the supernatural nature of the coming harvest of souls. He says, "the plowman will overtake the reaper." What does this mean? Picture this, the farmer is plowing the ground and sowing seed. As soon as he puts the seed in the ground, it blooms instantly, ready for harvest. The crop cycle is happening at such an accelerated rate that the reaper literally overtakes the plowman. Is he speaking of a literal agricultural miracle? No, he's using an earthly example to give us a heavenly reality. He's speaking about the acceleration of the gospel in the nations.

We are starting to see the early signs of this in some nations. The underground church in China has been exploding for years. An estimated 25,000 people come to Christ each day. Some estimate that China has about 200 million believers right now. The gospel is flourishing in India as well. It's estimated that someone comes to Jesus in India every seven seconds. We are also starting to see monumental breakthrough in nations where missionaries have labored for decades without any fruit. The underground church in Iran is exploding at a mind-boggling rate. There are an estimated two million believers in this predominantly Muslim nation.

Some friends of mine who have been working among unreached people groups in the Buddhist world are reporting unprecedented growth. A few years ago they hosted a seminar to train national leaders to plant house churches. On the last day of training they took a map and had everyone pick a region they wanted to plant churches in. The next year they hosted the training again and were hoping to have a few more pastors to train. To their surprise they had close to 400 people show up. They were amazed that there were so many new believers in this unreached area. However, they learned that these weren't just new believers, but the pastors of four hundred new church plants. In true Book-of-Acts style, the church had grown dramatically and exponentially. These stories are being replicated all over the world and it's only the beginning. This is the tip of the arrow for the worship and prayer movement! The restoration of the Tabernacle of David will unleash the greatest missions movement we have ever seen!

Global Revival

To say the church in the western world needs revival is an understatement. In pursuit of relevance the church has lost her counter-cultural grit. We've unwittingly absorbed the humanistic philosophy of the times and have reduced the gospel to a few weak self-help principles. Humanity doesn't need to be improved, it needs a complete overhaul. Transformation only happens through an encounter with the cross of Jesus Christ.

The nations are crying out for redemption. They are sick and in need of a healer. War, poverty, disease, terror, and perversion have ransacked and enslaved entire people groups while the Western church chases fantasies of bigger churches and bigger budgets. A sick church cannot heal a sick world! Powers and principalities have taken dominion over entire nations. These powers cannot be overthrown by better technology and programs. Satan's kingdom will only fall when the church rises! Our greatest days ahead will flow from the place of humble and persistent prayer.

The task of global evangelism cannot and will not happen until the church is awakened. Historically speaking, missionary movements are the overflow of revival. Amos predicts an end-time revival beyond our wildest imagination: "The mountains shall drip with sweet wine and all the hills shall flow it" (Amos 9:13).

Again, the prophet uses an earthly analogy to point to a spiritual reality. Wine is often used in scripture as a symbol of the Holy Spirit. When God poured out the Holy Spirit on the Day of Pentecost, the masses accused them of drunkenness. Alcohol couldn't produce this kind of impact; in a single day three thousand turned to the Lord.

Revival prepares the way for the harvest! The harvest is great, so the outpouring will be greater! He will give us everything we need to finish the job of global evangelization. This will be a revival that is far beyond a fascination with signs, wonders, and manifestations. The church will rise up in power, love, wisdom and creativity to reclaim the hardest and darkest places on the planet. The reality is, the church has hit a divine roadblock! We cannot proceed without another an awakening! We will not and cannot fulfill our divine mandate to disciple nations unless God pours out His Spirit again!

City Transformation
"They shall build the waste cities and inhabit them" (Amos 9:14).

Revival is not an end in and of itself! In revival God heals, re-stores and prepares us to be co-laborers in His dream to rebuild the ruined cities of the earth. There are cities and people groups across the globe that have lived under the tyranny of Satan's dominion for generations. The families of the earth are groaning under the weight of shame, hatred, bitterness, perversion and defilement. Principalities have remained virtually unchallenged for hundreds of years, giving room for advanced systems of evil to be built. Entire nations have been bound by poverty, racism, and perversion. Nation after nation have have been enslaved by demonic hierarchies and have failed to reach their God-given potential.

I'm not sure we even have language for this incredible promise yet: "They shall build the waste cities and inhabit them." I believe this is speaking of a day when the church will rise with unprecedented wisdom, creativity and power to disciple nations in the values and principles of the Kingdom. A great reformation will burst forth from the house of prayer causing broken socio-political systems to be dismantled and righteous foundations restored. I'm not advocating a restoration of theocratic government. I do believe ungodly rulers will continue to operate, but the church will make significant progress as they serve the cause of restoring the world. The church will be a well of strength and support in times of desperation and provide solutions that will lift depressed and impoverished regions of the world.

I believe we will see entire cities transformed, which will release its citizens to live in freedom, hope, and prosperity. What does it look like for an entire city to come under the dominion of Jesus as king? I don't believe the fullness of this will be seen in this age but we can't let this stop us from dreaming. We must apprehend everything available to us on this side of eternity. The kingdom is both now and not yet. We must labor to bring the kingdom now, realizing the fullness will not come until Jesus returns. God loves cities! Each one, even the worst of them, has a redemptive and holy calling before the Lord. God is awakening hope as we— through the eyes of the Spirit—see what's coming! In His presence, He will give us blueprints and practical wisdom for reforming and rebuilding ruined cities.

The Great Invitation

I've heard Lou Engle, founder of TheCall, say many times, "Prophecy is an invitation to intercession." We can't afford to take a passive attitude with prophecy. When God speaks, it's a call to war. We can't adopt the attitude that says, "If it's God, then I guess it will just happen." Prophecy is a call to partner with the living God. We have a role to play in world redemption.

The promises in Amos are descriptions of God's will and what's available to us. We must consume them until all cynicism and unbelief fall like scales from our eyes. God is not depressed in the least about the state of the world! Heaven is full of optimism because they are convinced of His sufficiency and power to restore fallen humanity!

We are the sons of God. He has given the earth to us as our inheritance! He is backing us up with His word and power. We must not bow to the spirit of the age and let rogue powers and principalities decide what will happen in our cities. Evil can only reign where we fail to take our rightful place. We must take up these prophecies like swords and fight with every bit of our might until the kingdoms of this world fall before the King of Glory.

Let the words of Amos 9:11–14 cleanse you of unbelief, heal your disappointment and awaken a childlike optimism that Jesus can and will take over the whole world with His love. Take this prophecy into the prayer room! Weep over it, proclaim it, and prophesy it over the dead and dry bones of your region.

Chapter 9

MADE FOR LOVE

David had a holy obsession for the presence of God. His life mission is summed up in his prayer,

> One thing I have desired of the LORD, that will I seek: That I may dwell in the house of the LORD all the days of my life, to behold the beauty of the LORD, and to inquire in His temple. (Psalm 27:4).

He made a vow to give himself no rest until he found "a place for the Lord, a dwelling place for the Mighty One of Jacob" (Psalm 132:2–5).

His yearning to be with God was the sole reason the Tabernacle of David existed. David's desire for God collided with God's desire for him.

Jesus expressed the core value of the Kingdom of God in His prayer, "Father, I desire that they also whom You gave Me may be with Me where I am, that they may behold My glory which You have given Me; for You loved Me before the foundation of the world" (John 17:24). Read that verse again slowly! You read it right, Jesus is full of desire and He wants to be with us! This is the entire point of the gospel. Love compelled Jesus to give His life to be with us.

Why Were You Created?

Her questioned lingered in the air, unanswered, creating a tension in my heart as I reflected on how to answer. She was a seasoned prophet, full of wisdom and insight and this alone was enough to intimidate me. Her question was a simple one, yet I knew she wasn't inviting me into a casual dialogue on things I was already schooled in. This was a teaching moment.

She repeated her question, "David, why did God create you?" I formulated at least three good responses in my mind: "To worship, to glorify God, and to win the lost." Before I could give an answer she made a profound statement that changed my life forever. She said, "God didn't create you to do anything for Him, He created you to be the recipient of His overwhelming, extravagant love. Your number one job description is to be loved!"

This wasn't just a nice thought. It was revelation—The Revelation. This is the very heart and substance of the Kingdom of God. God made us for love! This conversation worked its way through my heart over time. It challenged every ungodly thought pattern I built my life upon. It confronted every need in me to perform or strive to earn God's love.

Life Begins with Rest

The book of Genesis shows us God's original plan and the divine order of creation. For six days the great Artist spoke the world into existence. He created the earth first and then created man. For six days God labored and created the glorious wonders of the earth, all without the assistance of a human being. Why did He do this? Well, for one, God didn't need the assistance of man. I believe He did this because He was setting all of creation into divine order.

Think about it, man's first full day with God is the Sabbath—the day of rest. Adam began his life just being with and enjoying God. There was no agenda. There was no assignment. He didn't make man because He was desperate for workers to carry out His mission. God just wanted to be with His son. I can only imagine that Adam spent the day having his mind blown with the beauty and glory of the home God created for him. This is the foundational revelation of the Kingdom of God. Life begins with rest!

Your Job Description

God is love defined. He is not self-seeking, even in the slightest. He didn't make us with any ulterior motive. God is completely self-sufficient, because He is 100 percent perfect. We cannot add anything to God to make Him better, or take away anything to make Him any worse. He doesn't actually need us to do anything for Him. This is absolutely liberating. It frees us from the compulsion to achieve, perform and strive to be loved.

I really never understood the fullness of this until I became a father. When my wife and I dreamed about having children, we were never motivated to have them just so we could have more help with household chores—even though one day I hope this happens. I remember when our daughter was born. I must have stared at her for hours on end, never getting bored. My heart exploded with love and joy every time I looked at her. I would often tell her, "Your job description is to be adored and you are doing a great job!" The reality was, as an infant she couldn't give anything back to me and yet my heart was bursting with love for her. My love for her wasn't based on anything she could do or say to me. This is a glimpse of the divine!

As parents, our love is but a shadow of the pure and perfect love of our heavenly Father. He loves without condition, expectation or requirements. In fact, His love never changes, even when we do. He remains faithful, even when we do not! Our sin and brokenness cannot quench the fiery love of God. Our struggle with sin doesn't intimidate Him or cause Him to change His mind about us. In fact, He says "where sin abounded, grace abounded much more" (Romans 5:20). In other words, His grace will always outdo our sin. He is committed to us through every season of our souls. God doesn't expect us to be perfect and mature in every area of our lives as soon as we get saved.

If I expected my daughter to have the skills, manners, and attitude of a fully grown adult, I would constantly be frustrated with her. Because I love her, I honor where she is and serve her until she can develop, change and grow. This is exactly how God treats us. He's committed to fathering us, teaching us, and disciplining us as we go through the ups and downs of life.

Awakening Love

What is true love? The Apostle John defines it like this, "In this is love, not that we loved God, but that He loved us and sent His Son to be the propitiation for our sins" (1 John 4:9 ESV). Love doesn't begin with us, it begins with Him. God loved us, when we didn't love Him at all. He made the first move. He came to us in the middle of all our defiling sin and shame and said, "I choose you!" He isn't threatened, or intimidated by our darkness. He never turns His love for us off. When we understand how much He loves us even in our sin, shame and immaturity then it transforms us and awakens love. If you want more passion for God, meditate on His passion for you! His heart is the source that all love springs from.

I grew up in a very legalistic church as a teenager. I walked around in a cloud of guilt and shame all the time. I always felt an inward ache that I was falling short and needed to do more for God. So, like any good church boy, I worked harder to prove my love and to shake the guilt. As a sixteen year old I prayed two hours a day and read at least ten chapters of the Bible daily. This was my quota...just the right amount I needed in order to feel better about myself. I was miserable. I hated prayer and reading the Bible was a drudgery. But, I pressed on because I thought God expected that from me.

The reality was, I didn't know the love of God. If you had asked me if I believed God loved me, I would have definitely said yes. I had an intellectual knowledge of His love, but I hadn't experienced the depth of His love in my heart. In fact, I always felt that God was slightly annoyed and disappointed with me. I rarely felt the pleasure of His love.

Thankfully, God didn't leave me there. He pursued me! He put me in places and circumstances that confronted this false theology. Then it happened! The lights came on while I was reading John 3:16 on an airplane. I opened my Bible and it fell open to the world-famous passage John 3:16. I started reading, "for God so loved the world..." I almost turned to another passage thinking, "Oh, I've read that a million times." But I felt compelled to read it again. As I read, I was suddenly struck with the revelation that I didn't believe what I was reading. I read it over and over, but didn't feel any connection or life on what I was saying.

I don't know why, but this fierce determination rose up in me to keep reading this passage until I believed what it said. I personalized it as I whispered, "for God so loved me..." over and over. In between my repetitions I'd plead with the Lord, "show me your love" and confess, "I'm not sure I know you love me." Then about fifteen minutes into this, a veil was ripped off my eyes! I could see it! I could feel it—almost as if it was for the first time! The tears started to roll slowly at first and then began to pour like a river. It was like the very depths of my heart cracked open and a fountain of love poured out. Wave after wave of His love washed over me. It healed me, and delivered me, but most of all it awakened my heart to His love. Right there on a crowded airplane, sandwiched between two people God awakened love. I just kept whispering, "You love me, You really love me." The more I said it, the more my heart burned and the tears flowed.

The Culture of the Kingdom

Love is the core value of the Kingdom of God. God never operates outside of love. It's His one and only mode of operation. He will never bypass relationship just to accomplish His mission. Even the way God designed the human race to multiply testifies to this. God gave Adam and Eve a mandate to "be fruitful and multiply; fill the earth and subdue it..." (Genesis 1:28). The only way they could fulfill their destiny was by loving each other. Out of their intimate union and the overflow of their love, children would be conceived. It's absolutely stunning to think that love is the doorway of existence. This is how life was meant to be lived, in an atmosphere of unconditional love. We are born from and for love!

Love is the law, culture and substance of the Kingdom of God. Life breaks down when love is absent. Sin is the absence of love. All abuse, perversion and strife manifest when love is absent.

Love makes life work as God always intended it. Life can only reach its highest potential of greatness and enjoyment through love. Love makes life bloom!

Think about work. When you love what you do, it inspires creativity, excellence and sacrifice. Love fills our work with joy and unlocks new realms of potential. Without love, work can feel like a prison sentence. Just imagine if everyone absolutely loved what they did. What kind of world would we live in?

Every triumph of humanity was born from love and desire. Think about the greatest acts of courage, the most awe-inspiring works of art, and the movements that changed human history. What do they have in common? They were all inspired by and fueled by love. The greatest stories of human achievement, bravery and creativity can all be traced back to love. Love is the most powerful weapon against evil that we've been given. Love is the only force great enough to transform the human heart.

This is why God made family the key to dominion. God wanted us to fill the earth with families who lived and modeled the value system of the Kingdom of God. Family is the training ground for unconditional love. It's the place where we have the most opportunity to practice mercy and forgiveness. Family is heaven on earth. In family we mirror the unconditional love of God to one another. Our mutual acceptance creates the safety and freedom for us to mature, grow and ascend to our God-given potential.

The Divine Order of the Kingdom

When Jesus came, He blazed past the layers of complication that came through the law. The Pharisees had heaped heavy burdens on people's backs with hundreds of man made laws. There were those that gave their entire lives to studying the intricacies of this law-based living, but when Jesus came He reduced it all down to two main ideas: "Love God and love your neighbor! All the law and commandments hang on these two things" (Matthew 22:40).

This simple statement of Jesus is the substance of reformation. Jesus came to bring a revolution and to overthrow every system of man that wasn't born of love. He came to bring the superior Kingdom of love and restore orphan sons back to their Father's house. Jesus had a deep contempt for anything that wasn't born of love. Why? Because the absence of love is the root of all evil. For the spiritual leaders of His age to parade themselves as sons of Abraham and representatives of the Kingdom of God was absolutely disgusting to Jesus. He had no patience with them! He rebuked them, called them serpents and called them out every chance He got. Love is how we distinguish what spirit is at work in any person or group of people. Theological statements are not the test of whether something is of God—love is. Love is our litmus test in the Kingdom of God. If love isn't in it, it's not His kingdom, plain and simple.

Jesus taught us the divine order of the Kingdom of God. First, love God, then love your neighbor. The Tabernacle of David was a love revolution! It was a call to love God with all their hearts! As we return to the divine order of the kingdom, it will bring reformation to ungodly systems and practices in the church. The spirit of religion cannot breathe in a culture of love.

Everything Jesus did affirmed this divine order. Jesus started His miracle ministry at a wedding! Why did He do this? Surely there were bigger needs in the land. He could have healed a leper, cast out a demon, or raised someone's child back from the dead, but He didn't. He chose to reveal the glory of His Father's Kingdom at a wedding celebration by turning the water into wine (John 2:1–11). Jesus was preaching the core value of the Kingdom: it's about love! Marriage itself is one of the greatest pictures of Christ and the church.

"And He went up on the mountain and called to Him those He Himself wanted. And they came to Him, then He appointed twelve, that they might be with Him and that He might send them out to preach; and to have power to heal sicknesses and to cast out demons..." (Mark 3:13–15).

Here's the divine order of the Kingdom again. First Jesus called His disciples to simply be with Him, and then to go out and preach. Out of the place of intimacy and fellowship with Jesus they would do the incredible works of the Kingdom. This is the

Kingdom model and the priority! Our first call is to be with Him and to drink in His love. We actually have nothing of lasting value to give to people outside of intimacy with God. All ministry is love expressed. Evangelism, missions, worship, and serving the poor all spring from the well of God's heart. In the Kingdom, if we don't have love, then we don't have a ministry.

You don't need to teach anyone how to evangelize that has encountered the love and beauty of God. A preacher will never lack anything to say if he has beheld the glory of God on his knees. We can only give away what we have experienced. Ministry will be as easy and natural as breathing when love is our pursuit. We breathe love in and breathe love out!

Many great empires have risen and fallen using fear, control and violence as primary weapons. Those cultures end up caving in on themselves because fear always brings death and destruction. The only kingdoms that will endure are those that are built on the everlasting love of God. Love always produces life. It creates environments of honor and dignity where human beings can soar to heights of creativity and innovation. Love will change the world! At all costs we must get love!

The house of prayer is a prophetic sign to the church to return back to their first love. There are many important and pressing issues of our day, but our greatest pursuit must be the presence of God. The restoration of the Tabernacle of David is a love revolution. It's a call back to the divine order of His kingdom. Love will restore, reform and heal broken hearts, churches, organizations and cities.

Chapter 10

PRAISE: THE DOORWAY OF DOMINION

After flying for over twenty hours our team arrived at the airport in New Delhi, India only to discover we would be delayed another eight hours before we could continue our journey to the mountains of Nepal. Little did we know that our delay was a divine setup. I found a place to sleep while the rest of the team explored the gift shops in the airport terminal. I was rudely awakened by one of our students exuberantly telling me that our team had been invited to play music in a gift shop. We were excited! It felt like our mission trip had started before we had even arrived at our destination.

I laughed out loud as I entered the store. This wasn't an ordinary tourist trap—it was a store devoted to new age healing arts and Hindu spiritualism. Hindu idols and products promising spiritual enlightenment, true happiness and healing flanked every aisle. Right in the center of the room was a shallow wading pool with a sign that said, "healing pool." Health and wholeness were the promises for all who entered. In front of the pool was a small stage and on it sat an elderly, shirtless, turban-clad Indian man playing haunting eastern melodies on a flute.

As we arrived the manager quickly ushered us to the small stage to set up our instruments. Our strategy was simple: worship Jesus until His presence invades the whole shop! From the minute we strummed the first chord on the guitar, heaven seemed to open. The atmosphere was absolutely electric with the presence of God. Strangely enough, I felt more freedom in this New Age store than I have in many churches.

We sang our guts out and after about thirty minutes over one hundred people had gathered to see what was happening. God was moving so powerfully and we felt like the time was right to share the gospel and give an altar call. We invited anyone up for prayer that wanted to experience the presence of Jesus. To our surprise the the manager gathered every one of his employees to the front for us to pray for them. For the next two hours we prophesied, prayed for the sick and preached the gospel. I looked around at one point and saw person after person shaking and in tears as they experienced the love of God. We had the privilege of leading several people to the Lord that day. Praise built a highway for the King of Glory to extend His realm of influence over a group of people!

Enter His Courts with Praise

Praise is the first order of business in the Kingdom of God. Over and over the Bible confirms that when we approach God, we are to first "enter His courts with praise." When Jesus taught His disciples to pray, hallowing the name of God was the first activity on the list. There is nothing arbitrary about this order. God strategically placed praise as the first for several reasons.

God is Worthy

God is worthy of praise! The worth of God is enough reason for us to praise Him night and day. We don't need any other reason or motivation of personal benefits to declare that the King is worthy. If we never receive anything again from His kind and loving hand, He is still worthy. With that said, we must understand that God isn't a divine narcissist that demands some form of robotic praise. Praise isn't a one-sided activity, it's an invitation to a build a relationship. When Jesus taught His disciples to pray He said to pray like this, "Our Father who art in Heaven...." He's basically saying, "When you pray, call me Dad." Jesus teaches us that prayer is relational. He invites us to see Him and know this dimension of His nature.

Praise is a Vehicle for Encounter

Make a joyful shout to the LORD, all you lands! Serve the LORD with gladness; come before His presence with singing. Know that the LORD, He is God; it is He who has made us, and not we ourselves; we are His people and the sheep of His pasture.

Enter into His gates with thanksgiving, and into His courts with praise. Be thankful to Him, and bless His name. For the LORD is good; His mercy [is] everlasting, and His truth [endures] to all generations (Psalm 100 KJV).

Psalms 100 tells gives us the protocol for coming before Him. First it says, "come before His presence with singing, and know that the Lord is God." The psalmist makes a connection between singing and knowing God. Singing is powerful! It's a vehicle for an encounter with God. It's one of the few activities that engages both our intellect and our emotions at the same time. As we sing simple and powerful truths about God, the spirit of God reveals them to our hearts. Music sensitizes us and unlocks our emotions so we actually feel the One we are singing too. Singing moves us from an intellectual exercise into a living encounter.

God isn't interested in just teaching us facts about Himself. Facts don't change us: experience does. God wants to set knowledge on fire by giving us a full-blown encounter with His divine nature. He wants us to experience the full range of His emotions and personality. God invites us to see Him. This is how He builds a relationship with us. As we see His beauty, experience the fire of His love and feel the warmth of His affection for us, we move closer! This is exactly why Jesus taught us to start by hallowing His name. As we sing about the attributes of God, the Holy Spirit illuminates our words and helps us experience what we are singing.

Praise Transforms Us

Praise is all about His worth and glory. However, it's impossible to be in His presence and not change. When we experience the depth of His love and affection for us, it heals our broken hearts and changes the depth of our desires. When we stand before the fire of His presence it melts unbelief, drives out disappointment, and sets our hearts ablaze for more of Him. As we praise Him, we are awakened! We can't change the world until we have been changed first. This is why God invites us through the doorway of praise as first priority. He uses it as an agent of transformation and preparation for co-laboring with Him to extend the borders of His kingdom across the world. Praise is the doorway to dominion.

Praise Releases Faith

One of the greatest benefits of praise is that it unleashes crazy faith for the impossible. Several years ago I was facing a massive financial crisis. Anxiety overwhelmed me as I tried to figure out any way possible around it. As I prayed, the Lord instructed me to write down every financial miracle I could think of and to thank Him for it. I wrote down over one hundred miracles. I faithfully thanked my way through the list and by the time I got to number twenty, all my anxiety was gone and my faith was through the roof! By the time I reached fifty, I couldn't contain my joy; I danced and shouted all over the room!

Praise reminds us of the goodness and faithfulness of the Lord, which creates a hopeful expectation for God to do it again. I noticed something shift about halfway through this exercise. I went from thanking God for what He did (past tense) to what He was going to do! I literally entered into the joy of a breakthrough before it even happened.

Why is praise powerful? Praise is a conscious decision to take our eyes off our obstacles, or inward voices of intimidation to focus on the Lord. Whatever you focus on grows bigger in your mind. Psalm 34:3 says, "Oh, magnify the LORD with me, and let us exalt His name together." When we praise God, our view of God expands. In the Hebrew the word for *magnify* literally means to *nourish up*. When we praise God, we nourish or feed our view of Him. When our view of God gets bigger than our problems then we will experience breakthrough. Faith is the overflow of praise and faith is how the kingdom advances on the earth.

I believe this is one of the reasons that the Holy Spirit has raised up a night and day prayer movement. Until our view of Him gets bigger than terrorism, perversion, poverty and disease we will never be able to co-labor with Him to transform the world. God is calling us out of the shallows of unbelief, cynicism and hopelessness in order to sit and rule with Him in heavenly places. Through praise God calls heavenward to see as He sees and know as He knows. When we see Him it will awaken childlike optimism that Jesus is good enough and big enough to take over the whole wide world!

Praise Enthrones God

David built his kingdom around this simple revelation that God is "enthroned on the praises of Israel" (Psalm 22:3 NLT). Praise builds a throne for God in the earth. Does this mean that God ceases to be king if we do not praise Him? Absolutely not. Nothing can dethrone the King of Glory. He is and always will reign regardless of the loyalty and honor of human beings. However, He will only exercise His dominion in the earth where He is honored, welcomed and asked.

This is exactly why David built a massive throne of perpetual praise on Mt. Zion. As they honored the King of Kings, the Tabernacle of David became the very throne of God on earth. David teaches us that praise is God's primary vehicle for dominion. Through praise we give God jurisdiction over the realm He entrusted to us. In the midst of praise, God will answer our prayers, execute His judgments and expand heaven on earth. This was the key to David's success!

Praise Dethrones the Enemy

Praise opens the gates for the King of Glory to come in! When He comes, all inferior powers must bow before Him. Praise is one of our greatest spiritual weapons. As we praise, not only do we enthrone Him, but we also dethrone the enemy. These happen simultaneously. There can only be one King over our city. Praise is a choice to align ourselves with God's will and purpose. Agreement with God is defiance against the enemy. Satan only has jurisdiction where men's hearts are in agreement with him.

In praise, we never actually have to address the enemy in order to defeat him. As we build a throne for the King of Glory in our midst, all lesser powers fall before Him. Jesus uses the simplicity and foolishness of praise to crush the works of the enemy! "Through the praise of children and infants you have established a stronghold against your enemies, to silence the foe and the avenger" (Psalm 8:2 NLT).

Praise Drives Out Demons

When King Saul manifested demons of murder and rage, David picked up the weapon of praise. As he played his harp "the distressing spirit would depart from him" (1 Samuel 16:23). What made David think to do this? Think about this scene. One minute King Saul is in his right mind and the next minute he's cursing, contorting, throwing things and threatening to kill David. I don't know about you, but my first response wouldn't be to pick up a guitar and start playing. I'd either pick up a sword or run for my life. David's view of God was bigger than any enemy! In David's eyes, all opponents were inferior to God. He saw God defeat lions, bears and giants, why not a demon? David didn't turn to his own strength to defend himself. He turned to God in praise.

Praise Ambushes the Enemy

I love the story of King Jehoshaphat. It truly is one of the wildest testimonies of praise in the Bible. The news came to Jehoshaphat saying, "A great multitude is coming against you from beyond the sea" (2 Chronicles 20:2 KJV). Three enemy nations joined forces in one massive attempt to snuff out the entire nation. They were completely outnumbered and by all human accounts there was no hope. What did Jehoshaphat do? He called a prayer meeting. "He set himself to seek the LORD and proclaimed a fast throughout all Judah" (2 Chronicles 20:3 KJV).

We have a written record of what Jehoshaphat prayed at that prayer meeting. The first words out of his mouth were praise. He said things like, "You rule over all the kingdoms" and "no one is able to withstand you" (2 Chronicles 20:6–7).

What was he doing? He was reminding himself and all who gathered of the glory and power of the one that they were addressing. He was nourishing their view of God! The bigger the enemy the bigger our praise should be! By leading his people in corporate praise, he released a spirit of faith and confidence in God. It's interesting that he gave zero airtime to talking about the fierceness and size of their enemies in his prayer.

From the high place of praise, with his heart exploding with faith, Jehoshaphat came up with one of the most unorthodox military strategies of all time. I can only imagine what people thought when they first heard the plan. "We are going to do what? We are surrounded by hundreds of thousands of soldiers and you want us to...sing?" Yet, there's no recorded response of a revolt against this plan. No one shrank back or turned away. To people of faith, praise is a logical weapon against the enemy. In the midst of a national crisis, at the risk of losing their very lives, these men chose to sing to the Lord; to wield the greatest weapon of all time!

"And when he had consulted with the people, he appointed those who should sing to the LORD, and who should praise the beauty of holiness, as they went out before the army and were saying: "Praise the LORD, for His mercy endures forever" (2 Chronicles 20:21 KJV).

These soldiers stood on the front lines, stared death right in the face and sang to the King! When I envision this scene I always picture it like this: The men are gathered and dressed for battle, but instead of swords and clubs they have harps, trumpets and drums. They nervously look around, feeling vulnerable and foolish and then one brave soul among them finally begins to sing in a small frail voice, "Praise the Lord, His mercy endures forever." As he sings, others find their courage and join in. Soon a violent sound of praise roars through the valley, unleashing fear and confusion in the enemy's camp! Who could have imagined the response?

As they sang, God fought for them! "The LORD set ambushes against the people of Ammon, Moab, and Mount Seir, who had come against Judah; and they were defeated" (2 Chronicles 20:22). I think it's time we take singing armies into the heart of enemy territory!

Praise Creates Throne Zones

It was Saturday night and there were wall to wall people forcing their way through one of the most famous streets in America. People literally come from all over the world to party on the notorious Bourbon Street in New Orleans, Louisiana. The atmosphere invites people to throw off all restraint and dive deep into drunkenness and sexual perversion. For several summers the Burn 24-7 hosted a mission trip called the Burn Wagon. The vision of the Burn Wagon was to take teams across America in order to worship, pray and evangelize. The underlying philosophy is that God manifests Himself wherever we sing to Him! So we took worship to the hardest and darkest places in our nation to watch what would happen.

Our team pushed through the crowds, carrying hand drums and guitars seeking out the perfect spot to worship. It was so packed that they couldn't find any open spaces to set up. They finally sat on a curb, pulled out their instruments and started singing at the top of their lungs as people stepped on and over them.

The song was drowned out by the roaring masses and it seemed that no one was paying attention, but then something absolutely phenomenal happened. A perfect circle opened up in the middle of the dense crowd. People were literally crammed in this street, but when they saw the circle, they would walk around it as if there was an invisible force field. Then a man who was obviously intoxicated, stumbled into the middle of the circle. The presence of God fell on him and he collapsed to his knees weeping and began to worship God. A few guys prayed for him and led him to the Lord. As they prayed he was instantly and supernaturally sobered.

Then four young women who were celebrating a bachelorette party wandered into the circle and were also supernaturally sobered, gave their hearts to Jesus and were baptized in the Holy Spirit right on the street. This same scenario played out all night as people wandered into the circle and were overcome by the power of God. What happened? Their praises created a throne zone! Any inferior force that came into contact with His presence had to leave.

This story isn't meant to just hype you up with some charismatic lingo. This is a Biblical concept. God literally inhabits our praise. King Saul was driven by demons to murder David, but when he encountered the band of singing prophets he fell to the ground, ripped off his clothes and started prophesying (1 Samuel 19). What happened? He encountered the throne zone. When he stepped into the presence of God every inferior power had to bow. God is raising up singing prophets again to reclaim the ruined cities of the world! They have seen Him in His glory and are convinced of His ability to take over the whole world. As they sing, they set up throne zones and create atmospheres where men and women can encounter God.

I challenge you to go to the worst places of your city and shift the atmosphere through praise! Build a throne of praise right in the middle of the enemy's camp! Lift Jesus higher than every visible problem and invite God to bring His influence over that area and watch what happens. I did this with a group of interns a few years ago. Every Tuesday and Thursday we went to the same corner to worship and pray for two hours. Many times no one was there to hear us but we were faithful! Eventually things started happening. The results were astonishing! We saw the sick healed, drug addicts delivered and many come to faith in Jesus. There are people who prayed with us on that corner that are still faithfully pursuing God and attending the church today!

Praise is powerful! Our praise will build a throne for Him to come and rule and reign. There is no throne higher than His. No other principality can compete with the God of glory! Demons will flee, and ungodly power structures will fall as we lift up the name of Jesus! In praise we prepare the way for God to have jurisdiction and influence over our families, workplace and city! Praise the doorway of dominion! So open your mouth and open the doors for the King to come in!

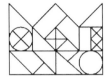

Chapter 11

HARNESSING THE POWER OF HOPE

"Blessed is the man who trusts in the Lord, and whose hope is the Lord" (Jeremiah 17:7)

We will not see revival, transform cities and win souls without hope! It is one of the most important ingredients to co-laboring with God to bring heaven to earth. Hope is the confident expectation that good is coming! It's not rooted in fantasy or pipe dreams but in the goodness of God. When we know His heart and what He has planned, then hope will naturally overflow! This is why prayer movements always precede revival movements. In the place of prayer God heals us of cynicism, unbelief and hopelessness. On the wings of praise, He lifts us into new realms where we can see what He's doing and hope can come alive! Why is hope important?

Those with the most hope, shape culture. Let me explain. The very fabric and substance of vision is hope. Anyone can have a great idea, but to really believe it will happen is what sets daydreamers apart from history makers. Visionaries don't allow the cultural climate or popular opinion determine the size of their dream or the intensity of their pursuit.

These hope reformers see the future long before anyone else does and exhaust all resources to see their dreams become reality. Visionaries think so big and so far ahead of the status quo that they are usually accused of being crazy. Yet it's those that have learned to harness the power of hope that change the world. Hope is the anchor of optimism in a culture of cynicism. Hope is the undeniable gut feeling that your dreams will change the world. It is a dreamer's fuel. It keeps you fighting for change, resisting discouragement and pressing in until your dreams become reality. Those who succeed at doing great things, refuse to feast on the voice of critics and self-doubt. Nothing great has ever been done by those who drink the lukewarm waters of the status quo.

What if Steve Jobs, the founder of Apple, never lifted his vision above the level of technology in his generation? In his day when computers weighed several hundred pounds and took up multiple rooms, his ideas for a personal desktop computer were absolutely revolutionary. Decades before technology could even realistically support his ideas, he was sketching pictures of the very first ipad. Most thought it couldn't be done and yet, here I am typing this book on a laptop computer more powerful than every computer put together in Steve's generation.

Dreamers see the future and pull it into the present. Their vision usually exposes areas of great deficit in the culture and for that reason they are greatly persecuted. Where would we be without culture warriors like Martin Luther King, Jr., who helped dismantle both cultural and systemic racism and prepared the way for the greatest days of racial equality in America? Dreamers live for a time not their own; they are the architects of the next generation. They have a value for generational momentum and see their efforts as just as important for tomorrow as they are for today.

If the world has learned to harness the power of hope for great secular and societal advances, how much more the church of the Living God? We have the most reason to hope! Our confidence isn't in the ingenuity of men, the benevolence of earthly governments or the might of the military. Our hope is in the unlimited resources of a loving and all powerful God.

Seeing Beyond the Headlines

The gift of revelation gives us the ability to lift our eyes above the current issues plaguing our world to see what God is doing. It doesn't take a prophet to see that things are not going well in the world. If that were the case then we could give this title to anyone who can read a newspaper. If we are not careful we can become so developed at seeing the problem of pain and evil that we can unwittingly foster a victim spirit and create a fear-based, reactionary culture.

This is not who we are! We are the sons and daughters of the living God. Dominion runs in our veins. We haven't been given the "spirit of bondage again to fear, but have received the Spirit of adoption by whom we cry out, Abba, Father" (Romans 8:15). The Spirit roars on the inside of us reminding us that the God of the universe is our Dad. The spirit of revelation gives us the ability to see God for who He really is! As we feast on His glory, power and goodness we inoculate ourselves against the principalities of intimidation. David put it like this, "The LORD is my light and my salvation; Whom shall I fear? The LORD is the strength of my life; of whom shall I be afraid?" (Psalm 27:1).

God invites us to see our city as He sees it. When we see what He sees, it awakens love, honor, and hope. I first began prophesying over cities on our summer mission trip called the Burn Wagon. Our team usually traveled to some pretty tough spots. One year we took our team to Salem, Massachusetts, which is notorious for witchcraft.

As we were approaching the city, I overheard several conversations about the legendary demonic activity and strongholds over the area. I could feel the fear and intimidation rising in people's hearts. Finally I stopped the van and told everyone to identify any negative feelings and thoughts they were having about Salem. I told them, "These are what Satan has done and is doing, now let's ask God to show us what He's doing." One by one students shared visions, words, and songs God gave them in regard to Salem. By the time we got to Salem our hearts were bursting with joy as we sang and chanted, "Jesus is the King of Salem!" When we saw what He saw, it delivered us from fear and released hope. In the few short hours we were in Salem we led people to Jesus, healed the sick and prophesied over dozens of people.

Prophecy Helps us See God Rightly

The primary role of the prophetic anointing is to reveal God to the human heart. "The spirit of prophecy is the testimony of Jesus" (Rev. 19:10). Prophecy testifies of and illuminates the beauty and glory of Jesus. Prophecy washes our eyes of every low-minded opinion of God and awakens hope! There is absolutely no hopelessness in heaven! Why? Because they see Him in all of His glory and power. I often picture the host of heaven worshipping God and then looking earthward as if to say "Do you see what I see?" He is holy! He is powerful! He is the author of life and holds the whole world together with the word of His mouth!" When we see Him it is impossible to be depressed. Hopelessness cannot survive in His presence.

Those who behold His glory will rise to confront the giants of culture without a shred of insecurity! He is bigger than terrorism! He's bigger than the porn industry! He's bigger than disease, abuse, poverty, depression and any other name that has lifted its fist against God. Jesus stands victoriously over all sin and death. He actually crushed them on the cross! Satan is not God's co-equal. He is a created being who will eventually bow his knee to Jesus! It is impossible to stay hopeless when you get a vision of who He is.

Fear produces apathy and an ungodly cautiousness. It causes us to live within the comfort zone of only what our strength and resources can produce. Fear clouds our minds from seeing who we really are in Christ. When we listen to fear, we reduce life down to only what's manageable. It creates a mindset that causes us to hide out in the safety of the four walls of our church. Hope on the other hand is aggressive! It sees the future and pulls it into the now. It doesn't wait for opportunity, it makes it! Hope has a revolutionary quality. It activates, mobilizes and incites movements!

Prophecy Awakens Warriors

Look at the story of Gideon. During his time the whole nation was under a spirit of fear and hopelessness. The enemy had raped and pillaged the land and left them with absolutely nothing. The once glorious people of God were reduced to hiding in caves and living in utter poverty. They would plant crops and as soon as it was harvest time, the enemy would burn the fields and destroy their food supply. In desperation "the children of Israel cried out to the Lord" (Judges 6:7), and God answered, but not in the way they expected.

In the opening scene we see Gideon hiding from the Midianites, threshing wheat in a winepress, and desperately hoping his meager resources wouldn't be stolen again. At the lowest point in his entire life, the angel of the Lord appeared to him and said, "The LORD is with you, you mighty man of valor" (Judges 6:12)!

Why did God say this to him? God was lovingly dismantling every lie that Gideon believed about himself and the Lord. He was inviting Gideon into one of the most important paradigm shifts of his life. "The Lord is with us?" Gideon must've thought this was insanity. Nothing about the state of the nation confirmed that the Angel was right. Gideon challenged the messenger's claim by saying, "If the Lord is with us, then why is all this happening? And where are all His miracles" (Judges 6:13)?

Gideon allowed his circumstances to define his theology of God. This is human nature. We all have done it at one time or another. When times get tough we question the goodness and even the presence of God. The accuser always shows up at these vulnerable moments to get us to doubt the goodness of God. A.W. Tozer says, "What we think about God is the most important thing about us." Our view of God determines our behavior. It's one of the most important battlegrounds we will fight on. If Gideon had eyes to see, he would have seen that God never left Israel, but was using the crisis to spark a national awakening. It wasn't until times got tough that Israel called on the name of the Lord and when they did, God answered!

It's interesting that the Angel never addressed Gideon's accusation. He didn't give this line of thought the time of day. The Angel cut right through Gideon's unbelief and spoke life to his identity when he said, "The LORD is with you, you mighty man of valor....Go in this might of yours, and you shall save Israel from the hand of the Midianites" (Judges 6:12,14). Gideon must have thought, "Mighty man of valor? Go in this might of yours?" Do you see me? I'm not mighty! I'm hiding in a pit! I'm weak and afraid!"

We tend to define ourselves by our weakness or our latest mistake, but God never does. God looks at the heart! He sees who He made us and called us to be and calls us into that. God wasn't flattering Gideon. He saw past all of Gideon's lies about himself and cut to the heart of the matter. God saw a warrior when Gideon saw a worm. God saw the flickering flame of courage, zeal and passion in Gideon's heart and called it out. God sent the messenger to wash his eyes from every inferior reality and awaken him to his destiny!

Gideon was pretty shut down. He needed God to confirm and reconfirm His word to him. We often judge people for putting out the proverbial fleece. But God is patient with us and will speak to us as much as we need in order to bring our thoughts into alignment with His. When His thoughts become our thoughts, then we will change the world!

When Gideon finally believed what God said about him, he acted accordingly. He did the unthinkable. He tore down the altar of Baal and put an altar to the Lord in its place. Even Gideon knew that the battle for nations is won in the place of worship. He dismantled the spiritual principality of the land and exalted God in its place.

His newfound courage was the manifestation of a fresh revelation of God and himself. We will always behave according to the view we have of ourselves. Our view of ourselves is the second greatest battleground the enemy will fight us on. He doesn't want you to see who you are in Christ. He knows that when you see who you are, then his days are over.

God's didn't answer Israel's prayer by sending a miracle, but by giving them a perspective shift. Think about this, Gideon had the solution to the nation's crisis beating inside of him the whole time. He had all the courage, wisdom, zeal, and power he needed to get the job done. What changed? His perspective shifted! He simply believed what God said and it awakened the warrior inside of him. He became the answer to his own prayers for deliverance.

Gideon became a prophet of hope to his generation. He called them out of their fear and apathy and awakened them to their destiny to take dominion over the nations. His courage incited a revolution! When it was time to fight, Gideon was not alone. Hope calls people out of fear and apathy and gives them fuel to fight for change! Hope begets hope! Courage begets courage! Awakened warriors, awaken warriors!

David's Prophetic Revolution

This is exactly why King David exhausted the first fruits of his wealth to build a resting place for the presence of God in the earth. He had the humility to understand He couldn't lead the nation apart from God's voice. When David came into power he inherited a mess! War, poverty and lawlessness almost wiped his people out. Thousands lost their lives in the war, King Saul had been slaughtered in battle, and the nation was leaderless and in despair. His people had reaped the harvest of a generation that had rejected the Word of the Lord. Saul despised prophecy, but David cherished it and elevated it a place of prominence in His kingdom. David went on a mission to build a culture of hope in the midst of calamity. He knew that if God's people would hope, then they would rise from their tragic past to build a glorious future.

This is why David appointed leaders whose number one job description was to lead prophetic worship. "David and the captains of the army separated for the service some of the sons of Asaph, of Heman, and of Jeduthun, who should prophesy with harps, stringed instruments, and cymbals" (1 Chronicles 25:1).

The captains of the army were involved in appointing the prophetic singers and musicians (1 Chronicles 25:1). Listening to God was David's greatest military strategy. He never made a move without inquiring of the Lord. Think about the soldiers sitting in the Tabernacle of David, having their hearts set on fire with the glory and greatness of God and then leaving that place to fight! The prophetic word was the fuel for the fight! Story after story confirms that when David asked, listened and obeyed, God gave them incredible victories. Legendary stories of David's exploits flooded the nations.

David created a prophetic culture in Israel. Night and day they postured their hearts to hear God's voice. For thirty-three years hope exploded under an open heaven. In one single generation Israel rose to a position of wealth and power that influenced the nations of the earth. By the end of his life, Israel enjoyed total rest from their enemies. The Tabernacle of David was a hope reformation! Their songs, prayers and prophecies awakened hearts, healed the land and elevated them to a place of global influence. Wisdom, creativity, and insight poured from Zion to the nations.

Prophecy awakens hope! It's one of the main reasons God has given us this gift! He wants us to see what He has planned, so we will get excited. These glimpses of the future are meant to awaken hunger and the will to fight. Prophecies are snapshots of future realities given to us as blueprints for building heaven on earth. We have a high calling to steward this prophetic anointing.

I believe this is exactly why the Spirit of God is calling us to night and day worship and prayer. In these presence-soaked environments He is delivering us of disappointment, and healing us of hopelessness. A new generation of hope reformers is rising from the flames of the restored Tabernacle of David! They are fueled by the optimism heaven and childlike faith that God is going to take over the whole wide world with His love.

Chapter 12

PILLARS OF POWERFUL PRAYER

I've sat through my fair share of boring prayer meetings. It's in those moments that I question the whole concept of prayer. Is God listening? Is this making a difference? Why does an all-powerful God need me to ask Him to do things He is perfectly capable of doing Himself? It's true, God doesn't need us for anything. If He did, He would cease to be God. He is completely self-sufficient. We can't add anything to make Him better or take anything away from Him to make Him any worse. He is absolutely, 100 percent perfect. He doesn't need us, but He does want us. Restoring the earth is His family business and He's invited us as His sons and daughters to partner in this grand adventure.

We are God's authority structure in the earth. He will not override our will to enforce His. If we don't want revival, He will not bring it. If we don't want His glory to transform our homes, families and cities, He will not enforce it. He waits to be asked!

Heaven is voice activated. He will not release the vast resources of the Kingdom of heaven on earth until we open our mouths. The spiritual realm moves at the sound of our voice. When we pray, angels move, demons flee and the will of God is enforced on earth. John Wesley summed up this idea when he said, "God never does anything in the earth except through believing prayer." It is mind blowing to think that the God of glory makes Himself vulnerable to the desires and the will of man. When our desires align with His, the Kingdom of God comes to earth.

In 2007 I was so hungry to be a part of what God was doing with 24-7 prayer that I started a house of prayer in my home. For an entire year, thirteen different worship leaders from a variety of churches led 20-plus hours of worship in my house each week. A small group of us committed to praying two hours in the morning and two hours in the evening. It was probably one of the craziest and toughest things I have ever done. Most of our prayer times were dry and difficult. I often wondered if our prayers were making any difference until something radical happened that changed it all.

I led a weekly prayer meeting focused on the Middle East. While I was preparing to lead my prayer time I learned that ancient Nineveh is the modern day city of Mosul in Iraq. As soon as I read this, faith came alive in my heart. I kept thinking, "Nineveh was saved in a single day! If God did it then, then He could do it again!" I came into my prayer time fired up and ready to storm the gates of hell for Mosul. Six others joined me as I sat down at my old, second-hand wooden piano to lead a few worship songs. About twenty minutes into our worship time, a violent spirit of intercession fell on me. It felt as if God took over my whole body. I went into a sort of karate-ninja-warfare mode as I pounded the keys and screamed in tongues at the top of my lungs. I had no idea what I was contending for, but I knew it wasn't just an emotional experience: God was up to something big.

When the dust settled and I came to my senses I started to become aware of how awkward I must have looked. I sat on the piano bench for a few minutes before I worked up the nerve to turn and face those in the room. When I finally turned around everyone was looking at me with wide eyes and open mouths as if to say, "What in the heck was that?" I just laughed and shrugged my shoulders. In my experience I don't always have the privilege of knowing what I am praying for when I pray in the Spirit.

The next day, I was browsing BBC online to see what was going on in the Middle East. I found an article that made me jump out of my seat. The headline read, "Iraqi security forces have arrested 74 people in a series of raids in the northern city of Mosul." The article stated that they had busted 74 terrorists and prevented two car bombs from going off on the very day that we prayed for Mosul! I was in absolute awe that God had used us to be a part of saving lives and changing history.

To read the full article go to:
http://news.bbc.co.uk/1/hi/world/middle_east/7903492.stm

If we only understood the weight of authority and power we carry in the earth! We are the gatekeepers of our generation! If we don't take our place, the enemy will. We have the power to write the headlines through our simple requests. We must shake off apathy and unbelief and let our voice be heard! The power of life and death is in our very tongues. I'd like to share with you foundational principles for effective prayer that I have learned over the last few years.

What is Intercession?

One of the greek words for intercession is *palal*, which means to intervene, intercede, mediate. In this context intercessors take the role of a mediator. We represent God to the earth and the earth to God. We stand before the Lord on behalf of those in need and we stand before those in need declaring that God will surely breakthrough. As intercessors we are the bridge between heaven and earth. We prepare the way for the earth to encounter the glory and presence of the Kingdom of God.

According to the Lord's Prayer, the goal of intercession is to bring the Kingdom of God to earth. The mission is to pray until it is "on earth as it is in heaven" (Matthew 6:10). This is God's will! God's deepest desire is that we would experience the same life, love and culture of His heavenly realm. Intercession is simply bringing our hearts into agreement with His will.

Preparing to Hit the Mark!

Another Greek word for intercession is *paga*, which means to hit the mark. I immediately think of an expert marksmen. Hitting the bullseye doesn't happen haphazardly, but comes through intentional preparation and discipline. God wants to train us to consistently hit the mark in prayer.

Most of what Jesus teaches us about prayer is preparation to strike the mark with precision. How we see God, and how we see ourselves are two of the most important components to effective prayer. Much of our prayer is about the journey of helping us see rightly. The Apostle Paul said that he prayed continuously that God would give the church "the spirit of wisdom and revelation in the knowledge of Him" (Ephesians 1:17). It's no wonder that the first part of the Lord's Prayer is about worship.

Praying as Sons

Jesus tells us to start our prayers "Our Father in heaven." The God of the universe is our Dad and it's His good pleasure to give us the Kingdom! When we pray this way, we put on the robe of a son and approach God as Dad. The revelation of the Father heart of God breaks the orphan mentality, which causes us to come to God to either prove or be approved. When we call Him Father we step into our positions as beloved sons and shake off the beggar mentality. What if we prayed with the revelation that God wants to bless, heal, restore and save the world way more than we do? It would change everything.

A few years ago I attended a church prayer meeting that rubbed me the wrong way. It took me a while to figure out why. On the outside it looked like a typical Charismatic prayer meeting: very loud and passionate. A few minutes into it, I realized that what bothered me was that their prayers sounded like begging. It was almost as if the people felt they had to pray loud and strong enough to convince God to do something good for them. If we don't know who we are praying to, we will pray amiss.

I used to live in South Africa and almost everyday people would come to our door begging for food or money. My mom would usually keep extra sandwiches or leftovers just in case someone came by. One day someone came begging and pleading with my Mom for food. While she was in the kitchen getting some food, I walked in right past the beggar and went straight to the refrigerator to get lunch. I had a different level of access because of my relationship. I was a son! I didn't need to beg and plead and say just the right words to get what I wanted. I knew who I was and what was available to me and I simply accessed it. When we understand who we are in relation to God it changes the way we pray.

Pray With an Expanded View of God

Before Jesus tells us to ask for anything Jesus tells us to pray, "Hallowed be Your name." The name of God is the full revelation and expression of His divine nature and personality. We will never pray bigger than our revelation of God. Listen to the way people pray and you will find out what they believe about God. By listening to some people you'd think that God was a weakling constantly on the run from the enemy. When we hallow the name of God we are simply telling God who He is and what He's like. Why does He ask us to do this? Firstly, because He's worthy, and secondly because our minds are renewed in the process. As we praise the name of God, the Holy Spirit will turn on the lights and give us powerful glimpses of Him. This is where faith and confidence come alive!

When we stand before the uncreated God and behold His infinite love and power our faith soars to new heights! When we see Him rightly, our prayers become saturated with divine optimism and wild faith that God is going to do great things. God invites us through the door of praise, so we will leave behind weights of fear, unbelief and hopelessness. Prayer is never more powerful than when it rises from the wings of praise!

The Tension Between Sorrow and Hope

Prayer sensitizes us to the both the heart of God and the plight of people. There are moments in intercession when God will let us feel the weight, the pain, and the sorrow of those we are praying for. There's something that happens in the place of weeping intercession that can't happen in any other type of prayer. This is where godly compassion is forged. Life and justice always spring from compassion.

In this kind of prayer our hearts become one with those we are contending for. Their pain becomes our pain. Their struggle becomes our struggle. As intercessors, we stand in the tension between sorrow and hope. On one hand we can feel the weight of people's problems and on the other we feel the hope that comes from simply trusting God. As intercessors hope and joy must be our default. We may have moments of sorrow but we always return back to joy. I generally find that if I carry sorrow outside the place of prayer it's not godly sorrow—but a ploy to pull me into heaviness and hopelessness.

We are not called to carry these burdens outside the place of prayer. If we do, it will crush us and make us needlessly vulnerable to spiritual attack and lies of the enemy. We don't have the emotional fortitude to carry the weight of the world on our shoulders. When we leave the place of prayer we need to simply hand these burdens back to God. It sounds simplistic to say this, but this simple prayer of giving the weight to God frees us to experience hope and joy for those we are interceding for.

The Synergy of Prayer and Worship

When Jesus cleansed the temple He declared, "my house will be called a house of prayer" (Matthew 21:13). He's quoting the prophet Isaiah. The Hebrew word for prayer in Isaiah is *tephillah*. This is an interesting word, there's actually no English equivalent. *Tephillah* is prayer set to music, or prayers that are sung. It's a form of prayer that engages both the intellect and the emotions. We are only beginning to understand the power and synergy of worship and prayer together.

In the early 1980s a worship movement exploded in the earth. Prior to that, there were very few worship recordings. Then suddenly, companies like Vineyard, Hosanna Integrity, and Maranatha started selling hundreds of thousands of albums. Books and conferences and training resources on worship started streaming in. Then, in the 1990s there was an explosion of teaching and resources on prayer. Movements like God's Generals and A.D. 2000 Prayer Track, Concerts of Prayer, and concepts like praying through the 10/40 window, spiritual mapping, and prayer walking emerged during this time. Yet, there was little to no teaching on revelation on the combining of worship and prayer together. In 1999 the International House of Prayer pioneered the Harp and Bowl model of prayer, which is the creative blending of scripture-based prayer with spontaneous choruses. Thousands of groups across the world have adopted this model of singing prayer and have reported that it is both an enjoyable and sustainable way to pray. But it's more than just enjoyable, it's Biblical!

"Now when He had taken the scroll, the four living creatures and the twenty-four elders fell down before the Lamb, each having a harp, and golden bowls full of incense, which are the prayers of the saints" (Revelation 5:8).

The heavenly model of worship includes both the harp and the bowl. The harp represents worship and the bowl the prayers of the saints. Worship and prayer were never meant to be separate. One serves the other. There's a divine synergy between the two. In worship God renews our minds, heals our hearts, and unlocks faith, hope and love. Worship prepares us to pray with an expanded view of God, from a deep well of love and with unwavering faith. When we pray from this place we will never miss! Worship changes us, but prayer changes the world.

Know What's Available

When you know what you have in Christ it changes the way you pray. A few years ago I saw a story on *The Oprah Winfrey Show* that blew my mind. A couple who had been struggling to pay their bills for years stumbled onto a website called lostmoney.com (not the real name). This site searches databases to find any money, stocks, bonds or land that descendants of yours failed to claim. This couple eagerly invested fifteen dollars to see if there was any unclaimed assets in their family line. To their shock they discovered an inheritance of eight million dollars that had gone unclaimed from over forty years ago. They had lived their whole life in poverty until they found out what belonged to them. Jesus has left us the incredible wealth of His Father's kingdom, but if we don't know what we have, we will never access it.

If I gave you five dollars to spend anyway you wanted, you would immediately limit all your options to what five dollars could buy. You'd walk around the store with a five-dollar mentality and probably come back with a whole lot of candy. But, what if I said, "Hey, my Dad just happens to own this store and said you can have whatever you want!" Well you'd probably head straight for the most expensive items. You'd probably get computers, TV's and furniture for everyone in your family including the dog!

The way you pray and what you ask for is directly related to what you know is available, too. Paul tells us that He is able to do "exceedingly, abundantly above all we ask or think" (Ephesians 3:20). Whatever you are asking for right now is probably too small. We usually only pray for things that we can accomplish in our own ability. But our Father is unlimited and it's His good pleasure to give you the Kingdom of God. When we see Him rightly and what He's provided, our prayers will explode! We will begin to dream with God about taking over entire cities, discipling nations, curing cancer, eradicating poverty!

You Are an Owner, Not a Renter

There was a time that I walked around my town and prayed over it every day. I remember getting the wild revelation that my city belonged to the Lord. I began to envision God taking over entire city blocks. One day while walking and praying, I said, "God what do you want to do with our city?" I was totally shocked by what God said. He said, "What do you want to do with it, I gave it to you as an inheritance!" This absolutely blew my mind. I realized that I had always had a renter's mentality in regard to our city.

I've been a both a renter and an owner of a home and they are two totally different experiences. When I rented, I had to accept the house as it was. I didn't have the freedom to paint, renovate or make any structural changes. But when I bought a home, I had the right to do whatever I wanted. I began to dream about all the things I could do to make my home a custom fit for my style and needs. Ownership unleashes creativity! When you understand that "the earth is the Lord's and all its fullness" (Psalm 24:1) and that He has given it to us as an inheritance, it changes the way you pray.

We must war against any mentality that makes us think we are servants to the whims and wishes of the enemy. We are not His tenants! We are the rightful rulers of the land! When I started thinking like an owner I began dreaming wildly about the greatest days our city has ever seen. It blew the ceiling off of my heart! It unlocked a well of creativity for both reaching and restoring the land.

The reality is that you have been sovereignly placed in your city by the Lord. You are the answer to the problems plaguing in your city. Your city belongs to you and if you don't take your position of the authority then the enemy will fill the vacancy. God has endowed you with all the power, authority and resources you need to help your city reach its full potential. The enemy cannot rule where the children of God take their place.

Prayer is More Offensive than Defensive

Intercession is the language of hope. It finds its highest expression in what it is fighting for, not what it's fighting against. Fear and worry often knock on the door of your heart disguised as a burden of intercession. If we are not careful we will get distracted by our so-called discernment and miss what God is doing. Our prayer lives should be fueled more by what God is doing, rather than what the enemy is doing.

This is a very important shift in thinking when we are learning to pray effectively. Prayer is more offensive than defensive. To be defensive in prayer is to take the weaker stance. Offensive prayer is built on the revelation that God has already defeated the works of darkness! We have to get delivered from the fortress mentality that says, "hunker down and pray for the best." Jesus won, so we are on the winning team! We are God's authority in the earth and we set the agenda.

Often times I find we are overdeveloped in our ability to discern evil. Ask any intercessor and they can readily tell you the names of the principalities and strongholds over their region. There is a place for understanding these things, but these should never

set the course for our prayers. When we focus on evil, we tend
to primarily be reactionary and defensive in our prayers. Our
true calling is to discern what God is up to in our city and pray
that!

If the primary focus of our intercessory burden isn't a vision for
life and doesn't carry a spirit of optimism, then it's not from God.
The atmosphere of heaven is charged with hope. Hope is the
overflow of the revelation of both His greatness and His
goodness. Hope is the fuel that gives us the energy and
motivation to build His kingdom in the face of resistance. Those
who carry the torch of hope will change the destiny of cities and
nations.

We Pray the Word to Hit the Mark

God has given us a fail-safe way to strike the mark every time
with our prayers and that is to pray the Bible. The Word of God
contains the will of God. When we pray the scriptures we cannot
miss! Praying the Word always points to the precise target on
God's heart. His Word is the final authority. There is no
principality that can stand against the Word of God. It is the
most powerful weapon we have in our spiritual arsenal.

Love is Our Authority

When I first started praying for the church in our city on a
regular basis I had a lot of pride. I often prayed from a sense of
spiritual superiority—a sort of "us and them" mentality. We
were the fiery worshippers and intercessors losing sleep for the
cause of revival and they were the lukewarm, apathetic,
religious church who could care less. The truth is, much of the
negative things we saw happening in the church was true.
However much of what we called discernment was actually
judgment. When we spend time in prayer, our discernment will
be heightened and we will see things that are out of order.
Discerning sin isn't the problem, it's what we do with it that
counts. If love isn't present, then our discernment can lead us
into judgment. Love always pulls people to us like a magnet but
judgment repels.

God was patient with me as He taught me the heart of a true intercessor. One day after a moment of frustration with the church in our city, God spoke to me and said, "Are you not a part of the church you are criticizing? How can you separate yourself from the body I placed you in? You are the church and the church is you. Their sin is your sin. Their pain, your pain. Their joy, your joy!" The blinders were ripped off of my eyes! I saw myself as one with this gloriously messy bride! God spoke to me and said, "Are you willing to wash the feet of my Bride?"

The heart of the intercessor is to take the towel and basin and wash people with our prayers! This is the heart of Jesus. He didn't come to earth to flaunt His superiority over the poor, sinful earthlings. He came and sat in the dirt with us! He met us where we were and pulled us out of the pit with His love. Isaiah puts it like this: "He poured out His soul unto death, and He was numbered with the transgressors, and He bore the sin of many, and made intercession for the transgressors" (Isaiah 53:12 NIV). Jesus never sinned one time, but still numbered Himself with the transgressors. He counted Himself among the many thieves, murderers, and adulterers. Their sin became His sin. He owned it, He felt the weight of it, and wept over it and from this place He "made intercession for the transgressors."

Judgment and love cannot co-exist. In order to pray effectively we must cleanse our hearts of all judgment and pride. Love is the ultimate source of authority in the Kingdom of God. Love is what sets apart the Kingdom of God from the kingdoms of men. We cannot have true influence over anyone or anything we don't love. I believe this is one of the main reasons that God chose to make intercession a key to taking dominion. In the place of prayer He lets us feel His heart for those we are praying for.

Becoming the Answer to Your Prayers

Be careful who you pray for! God may send you to reach them. Think about it, what better people to send to the harvest fields than the ones who have sat in the place of prayer and had their hearts lit on fire by the love of God for the lost. I sat in a prayer room for an entire year praying for the Middle East every

Wednesday. When I first began my journey in prayer, I didn't love the Middle East. In some sense I wanted them to know Jesus, but I really didn't love them. However as I prayed for them week after week I started to see them as God saw them. I started to feel their pain and identify with their burdens. At one point I couldn't open my mouth in prayer without weeping over them. God gave me a deep love and respect for a people I had never met, in the place of prayer. One year later, I found myself stepping off an airplane into the blazing desert sun of Northern Iraq.

I went with a team to start the very first Burn Furnace in this vastly unreached nation. We hosted twenty-four hours of continuous worship and prayer in an Iranian house church on our first few days there. I believe our fervent prayers for the Kingdom of God to come to Iraq plowed the way for the massive breakthrough we experienced while we were there.

Through a series of divine connections we were asked to lead worship in one of Sudaam Hussein's former fortresses. This was one of the places where they boiled thousands of Kurdish settlers alive during the genocide. It was very surreal to be invited to this place. We teamed up with a group of missionaries who were hosting English classes there. While the soldiers were taking tests we sat on the balcony playing music to those waiting. Dozens of fierce-looking Khaki-clad soldiers packed in around us as we sang simple worship songs.

At one point while I looked up into these soldiers' eyes, the Spirit of God began to sing through me! I started singing prophetic songs over them and declaring things like, "You and your house are going to come to Jesus! You are going to know His kindness and love!" Most of them couldn't understand what I was singing, but tears began to well up in their eyes. Later, one of the soldiers told us "You have made this sad place a place of great joy and refreshment." They had an encounter with the presence of God, and it changed the atmosphere.

I noticed a young man with a professional grade video camera recording the entire worship time. Later he explained that he was getting footage to put this on the evening news. We were so excited that our little worship time would make the evening news. Yet this was nothing compared to what was getting ready to happen. The next day, we got a call asking us to do a concert at the fortress for soldiers and their families. When we arrived, they led us through the courtyard to the place where the concert would be held. I pictured us all sitting on the concrete floor with our guitars with a handful of men with their families joining us. So, when I walked into the room I was totally shocked. There were probably about three hundred people in attendance, concert lights, tv cameras and a fully equipped concert stage! They ushered us in like we were rockstars, with people recording every second of it on their cell phones.

When we took the stage the Spirit of God took over! We sang, prophesied and declared the Word of God while a translator interpreted key moments. At the end of the session, our leader looked over at me and said, "Play one more song." I panicked and my mind literally went blank. Finally the only song I could think of was the 1980's Hebrew-style worship song, "When the Spirit of the Lord." Little did I know that the beat and minor scale the song is written in was the closest match to the sound of their traditional music. They went wild! They kicked chairs out of the way, linked arms in a giant circle and began to dance! We had a wild party as the presence of God released joy over the whole place. After the meeting they told as that our worship time had been broadcast live all over Iraq, Iran and Turkey! We were in absolute awe that God had opened a door for us to preach the gospel all over the Middle East.

At the end of the meeting we were told that the Prime Minister of the Iranian Democratic Republic was in attendance. This group has been fighting for freedom and democracy in Iran for over thirty years. They told us that he wanted to meet with us the next day. Part of me was worried that we were in trouble. I mean, we preached the gospel to Muslims on international television. When we arrived to his office we were greeted by servants in white gloves and were offered trays of fruit. It was clear we were in the presence of a dignitary.

He began to tell us how thankful he was that we came. He said that when he heard our music it reminded him of an American rock group that went on a goodwill tour to Cuba during the height of the war against communism. He went on to say that many criticized this group but their music was a key that opened the door for talks between Cuba and the West. Then he said something I'll never forget. He said, "When I heard your music, I knew it was the key that would open a door for our people to get help." Little did he know he was prophesying the future of his people. We told him that we could bring back medical clinics and other forms of aid, of which he was very thankful. Then, one of our guys spoke up and said, "We want to bring as much help as we can, but we also want to tell your people about the greatest man that ever lived. Could we teach your people stories and songs about Jesus?" He joyfully replied, "Anything you bring to us, we will take!"

Several months later we brought the promised medical clinics and saw over two hundred people give their lives to Jesus and dozens healed. Today, in that very place we have a long-term team that continues to minister to both the practical and spiritual needs of the people. It all started with a prayer! As we prayed, God took us on a journey! He gave us faith, hope and love: all the ingredients we need to change the world!

Prayer changes us and we change the world! This great prayer movement is preparation for one of the greatest breakthroughs in global missions we have ever seen. From the fires of intercession, missionaries will be thrust forth into the hardest and darkest places in the earth. Their hearts beat with optimism of heaven! They are convinced that God is good enough and big enough to take over the whole world! They are fearless in the face of death, persecution and evil. Their relentless love for the lost compels them to fasted lifestyles and sacrificial living. They believe like children, but fight like kings. These are the great end-time intercessory warriors!

Chapter 13

TRAINING FOR REIGNING

Our future is bright! We have been set up to succeed! We are standing on a mountain of scriptural promises, prophetic words and decades of prayer for the coming wave of revival and harvest. Our kingly mandate to bring the culture of heaven into every sphere of society is a high and costly one—one for which we are not ready yet. The reality is, if God were to give us the fullness of what we are praying for right now, it would crush us.

So, in His mercy He will take us through a training regiment to get us ready. Before we can reform culture we must undergo an inward reformation. This training has very little to do with what we think it does. It's not about improving or developing skills, it's about the heart. Your heart is the doorway of the Kingdom of God in the earth. Therefore, God will pursue your heart above all else! He will lovingly take us through the furnace of hardship until anything not like Him is melted away. He will deal with the inward world of values, motivations, character and mindsets. The condition of our hearts is what qualifies or disqualifies us to reign with God in the earth.

Hardship—The Boot Camp of the Kingdom

Do you ever feel as if you are in perpetual transition? Do you feel like you are facing constant challenges at home, at work, and ministry? Congratulations! You are in training for reigning. God uses all the pressures of life, spiritual warfare and relational conflict to build you into the person you are called to be! God isn't doing this to crush you or kill you, but to prepare you for stepping into your wildest dreams. Hardship is the boot camp of the Kingdom. Why does God do this? It's only in fires of testing that we truly see what's inside of us. God is committed and faithful to us in this process.

David is one of the best examples of how God prepares us for positions of authority and influence. He was anointed to be king as a teenager, but it wasn't until he was thirty years old that he took the throne. When Samuel poured the horn of oil over his head as a young shepherd boy, David wasn't ready to reign. Between the sheep pen and the throne room were twenty years of trials and testing that prepared David to be King. God took those years to forge in David the qualities and character needed to co-rule with God in the earth.

We are called first be priests and then kings. This is the divine order of God's Kingdom. God trains us for kingly influence by first preparing us to walk in our priestly anointing. The priestly call is about aligning our entire life and value system around the presence of God. In this season, God confronts all of our other lovers and exposes anything we've built our identity and lives around. Unfortunately the priestly anointing is cultivated through hiddenness and hardship. Before David ever had a title or any influence he was hidden away tending sheep in the hills of Judah. Before He was a king, he was a worshipper. This was the place he discovered the point of life and fell deeply in love with the King of all kings.

Training In Humility

One of the first qualities necessary to reign with God and to ultimately fulfill our destiny is humility. Jesus put it like this, "Blessed are the poor in spirit, for theirs is the kingdom of heaven" (Matthew 5:3). To be poor in spirit is a constant and painful awareness that we need God. It is a healthy self-aware-ness of our weaknesses and shortcomings. Those who are poor in spirit have both an overwhelming revelation of the goodness and power of God and their desperate need for Him. Poverty of spirit is not shame. Shame is destructive, because it tells us we are too wounded and broken to change. But poverty of spirit is full of hope because it leads us to the only one who can heal, change and fill us up!

It's only when we have enough humility to embrace our weakness that we will ever truly call on the name of the Lord. So, in God's mercy He will remove the awareness of His presence or delay an answer to prayer to remind us of what it feels like to do life without Him. These seasons of hardship aren't meant to kill us, but to kill our pride. Pride destroys our appetite for God, because it deceives us into thinking we can live life outside of God's presence. Jesus tells us that "the Kingdom of Heaven belongs to the poor in Spirit." Poverty of spirit is the key that opens the door to the wealth, wisdom and power of heaven!

Saul was the the example of what not to do! Saul's life shows us that God will not cooperate with hard-hearted, prideful, and rebellious men. Humility attracts God. He resists the proud, but gives grace to the humble. David went through the school of humility. He lived a good portion of his life on the run, living in caves, stripped of position and title. When David became king he was broken and humble. Everything about how David led was bathed in humble dependence on God. The tabernacle of David was a manifestation of his humility. He knew that he couldn't live or lead God's people outside of God's presence and guidance. Lessons in humility are the first phase of priestly training.

Now, what I'm about to tell you next comes with a warning label! Don't do this unless you know that you know it is God. I'm not advocating my testimony as a model to be followed or as some sort of badge of spirituality. With that said, here we go: When I graduated from seminary, I had it all figured out. I thought I had the golden keys for revival and church growth and was ready to prove myself. I felt like God told me to quit my job as youth pastor to seek him for the next season! I really thought doors would fly open and I'd step into all my prophetic promises to change the world. However, as I prayed about my future, God was strangely silent, and as time went on, no doors opened. It was like someone suddenly turned off the lights!

I started to panic a bit because I had given up my only source of income. I went to the park every day to walk and pray—or should I say, walk and worry. I was disoriented and couldn't figure out what God was up to. When God finally broke the silence, the only thing He said to me was, "I don't want you to work until I tell you to." What? This couldn't be God, I thought. The Bible says, if you don't work, you don't eat. So, I started a job search and not one person would hire me. I had just graduated with a Master's Degree and not one person would give me the time of day, not even for an entry level position!

Finally, in desperation I went back to the Lord and told Him, "If this is you, then you have to provide...because I'm freaking out." Suddenly, money started coming in from weird and random places. I never told anyone about what God said. I wasn't putting out "faith hints" or carefully crafted fundraising letters. There I was, at the mercy of God. I'd frequently run into people I went to school with and they'd ask, "So, what are you doing now that you have graduated?" I'd painfully and awkwardly answer, "Nothing." They'd always say something like, "Oh, so where are you working?" and I'd sheepishly reply, "Nowhere." I didn't feel any sense that I was spiritual because I was living by faith. I felt humiliated. I was hearing about the amazing opportunities and jobs my peers were getting and here I was with no job, no ministry and no title.

I didn't know it at the moment, but I was exactly where God wanted me. God was radically reorienting my entire value system. He was calling my identity out of what I did and compelling me into the secret place to develop my priestly call. God exposed my idols of ministry, titles and education during this season. I had never seen how I had used these as crutches. I had no idea how much these activities were intertwined with my identity. In some ways I forgot who I was apart from them. It was painful to see where I really was, but absolutely necessary for what God was doing in me. For the first time in years, I had absolutely nothing to do with my time, so I pursued God with everything in me.

I turned my tiny bathroom into a house of prayer. I set up a music stand in the bathtub and sat on the toilet with my guitar and sang and prayed for hours a day. Those first few weeks in prayer were pretty dry. I realized that I didn't know the Lord like I thought I did. I was extremely busy with school and ministry and only prayed or studied when I needed to prepare for a sermon. But God began to reveal Himself to me in profound ways. It wasn't long before my dull prayer meetings became rivers of refreshing. I was falling in love with God and couldn't get enough of His presence. My heart was being softened and coming alive as God began to reveal the depth of His love for me. I spent many days weeping over familiar passages like the Lord's Prayer or John 3:16. God kept me in this place for almost a year.

By the end of this season I came to the point where I told God, "I don't care if I ever do anything for You again, I just want to be with You!" My confession was an expression of the radical reformation of heart that I went through during that year. God set my life on the right foundation! He trained me in the priestly anointing by calling me away and teaching me how to know Him in the secret place. When I look back, I am overwhelmed with gratitude that the Lord saw fit to take me through this. I would have been extremely dangerous and full of pride had I not confronted my barrenness and gone the way of the wilderness. It was both the toughest and most glorious season of my life to date.

Training in Meekness

"Blessed are the meek, for they shall inherit the earth" (Matthew 5:5).

The next heart quality required to reign with God is meekness. What is meekness? It's often translated as gentleness of heart. Throughout scripture, meekness is almost always talked about in the context of hardship or accusation. Meekness is the ability to keep a soft and open heart in the midst of hardship, conflict, and accusation. David endured incredible accusation and conflict with Saul, but never hardened his heart. Meekness has the idea of strength under restraint. In other words, those who are meek choose not to use their power and influence to hurt and destroy others. Saul did so many incredibly horrible things to David. He would have been justified to use his strength and influence to destroy Saul, but he never did. He showed incredible restraint in the face of persecution.

The promise to the meek is that they "will inherit the earth." Humility gives us authority in heaven, but meekness gives us authority in the earth. The meek will impact and influence the earth. Meekness is what gives us favor and an open door with people. Without this, we will never have impact. I love that in the Kingdom of God you cannot influence men without meekness. Meekness is the ability to keep our hearts open and soft in spite of hardship and conflict. It's easy to stay open and soft toward God because He's perfect. But when dealing with people, that is hard! They can be mean, purposefully hurtful and self-seeking. I remember hearing a pastor say, "I'd love ministry if it wasn't for people." This is funny, but really true for a lot of us. If we aren't careful we will close and harden our hearts to the very people we are called to serve.

The reality is we need each other. God uses people's immaturity, sin and weakness as a tool of transformation in our own hearts. The meek have fought to keep their hearts open in the middle of pain. The reality is, people will hurt, disappoint and dishonor you. It's what you do with the pain that counts. The meek heart is an open heart. When you live with an open heart you risk getting hurt. King David wrote songs about it. He sang lyrics about crushing the jaws of His enemy and trampling them under feet. He kept his heart open by venting his hurt and pain to God.

Forgiveness is the daily practice of the meek. It's the only way to keep our hearts soft and open. If we let unforgiveness grow, then bitterness will defile every single thing we touch. We will never be able to effectively work with or minister to people unless we fight to keep our hearts free of bitterness. Unforgiveness ultimately hardens the heart and causes us to build walls in order to protect ourselves from people. The call of the meek is to live open, soft hearted and vulnerable. When our hearts are open we have the most impact! We cultivate a sense of authenticity and safety that attract people to us.

Training in Honor

David was a man of honor. This is one of the most important qualities of a king. He had every right to destroy Saul's name to everyone he knew, but he never did. In fact, when Saul died, he wrote a song titled, "Song of the Bow." It is an incredible tribute to Saul. It starts by saying, "The beauty of Israel is slain on your high places! How the mighty have fallen!" (2 Samuel 1:19).

A few years I go I planned a citywide worship gathering. I spent weeks meeting with pastors and worship leaders to get the word out. I prayed, fasted and really believed God to unite the churches in our city and when the event came almost no one showed up. On top of that the host pastor treated our guest impolitely and treated us as if we were a bother to their church. I was so upset! I had so much judgment and accusation rolling through my heart.

In the middle of all of this, God spoke to me and said, "The church will not be built unless they can honor." I chose to forgive this pastor and release him from any false expectations I had. In that moment I had a vision of myself suspended above our city. I saw key churches with labels over them like, "prophetic, evangelism, pastoral, apostolic and teaching." I immediately knew that these were anointings that these churches excelled in. In the vision there were high walls around these churches called suspicion, judgment, dishonor and pride.

Then God spoke to me and said, these churches have matured in their own anointing but haven't risen to the place of wholeness, maturity and impact because they have built walls of dishonor towards others in the body of Christ. It was so clear to me. Each church had excelled in their own gifting and used this as a tool of measurement for everyone else. For example the prophetic church was criticizing other churches for not being more prophetic. Then I saw the church honoring each other and when they did the walls fell and bridges were built and people were streaming in and out of other congregations. Honor gave them access to one another's anointings. When the walls fell, the five-fold anointing flooded the churches causing them to all grow and rise higher.

Jesus teaches us that we can only receive from those we honor. He said, "He who receives a prophet in the name of a prophet shall receive a prophet's reward" (Matthew 10:41). When Jesus came to His hometown, they were so blinded by His humanity that they couldn't see His divinity. When they heard about the miracles their first response was, "Isn't this the carpenter's son?" Their dishonor kept them from receiving His anointing. It says that "He did not do many mighty works there because of their unbelief" (Matthew 13:58).

Honor gives us favor with man! We cannot accomplish our mission without favor. We can prophesy all day long, and shred principalities, but if our love for God doesn't translate to genuine honor for people then doors will always be slammed shut in our face.

We have this insane idea that when revival comes a glory cloud will hover over entire cities and people will call on the name of Jesus. However, the kingdom of God will be expressed through you! God will not override human relationships to bring the Kingdom of God. Genuine honor and respect will open the doors for people to know God. Honor builds bridges between people. It creates an atmosphere where people feel like the best versions of themselves. Honor is the atmosphere where people reach their full potential.

Humility, meekness and honor are the three qualities necessary for us to grow in our priestly and kingly call. We cannot reign with God without these three. When David finally took the throne he had been through the school of humility, meekness and honor. These qualities gave him the ability to reign with God and to extend the empire of heaven to the ends of the earth.

Kingdom Reformation

Prayer movements always precede revivals! Why is this? For one, God won't bring revival unless we ask. Second, it's during the seasons of faithful and persistent prayer that God forges in us the heart of those that can reign with Him. He purifies our motivations, heals our hearts, and delivers us of any mindsets that hinder what God wants to do. Revival is a return to truth and truth is the substance of reformation. When the revived rise up to wield the sword of truth it will level broken systems and rebuild church and society upon the eternal foundations of the Word of God.

David's Tabernacle is not a call to a movement or a model of ministry, but a return to the Kingdom as God always intended it! The Davidic reformation brought Israel back into alignment with the divine order of the Kingdom. David taught us that our first and highest calling is to be priest and then from this place we reign as kings. David built an entire culture and governmental system around the priestly call to minister to the Lord through worship, praise, thanksgiving and intercession. As God was enthroned in the praises of His people, He extended the authority over the nations. Israel stepped into their kingly authority as they rose to a place of unparalleled prominence and power in the nations in just one generation!

The Tabernacle of David shouts to us from the halls of history to forsake our man-centered, celebrity-driven culture and seek the one thing that matters—His presence. At its very core it is a call to His face, to build our lives, ministries and churches around the glory of His presence. If we make this our primary pursuit, if we conform to this kingdom pattern, then the gears of transformation and reformation will begin to turn in our generation. Ancient strongholds will fall as the church rises up in her identity and authority. Ungodly systems and structures will be dismantled in both the church and the secular arena as we take our place.

We will rise as hope reformers to rebuild the ruins of culture and set society back on godly foundations. People groups will be reached and entire nations will be discipled in the ways of the King and His kingdom.

About the Author

As a third generation revivalist, David Fritch carries a rich heritage for worship and intercession. He has a Masters of Theology from Regent University and a passion for truth and equipping the body of Christ with the hope and freedom of the gospel.

David has been serving Burn 24-7 over ten years and is the Founder and CEO of "Thinkable", a Learning Management System. He currently resides in Virginia with his wife Heather and their two kids.

Other Books by Author

Burn 24-7: A Collision of Vertical Worship and the Great Commission

Culture of Revival, Vol. 2

Fuel for the Burning Heart, A Daily Devotional

Connect with Author

I really appreciate you reading my book!

If you would like to invite me to speak or teach at your event please contact me through my website. Here are my social media and website information:

Facebook: https://www.facebook.com/davidfritchministries/

Twitter: https://twitter.com/Davidfritch

Website: http://www.davidfritch.com/

Website: http://www.burnfieldtraining.com/

Email: davidf@theburn247.com

Thinkable Learning Management System

Do you have a desire to put your courses, school or training online? Look no further! Thinkable is the solution for you! This is an easy-to-use platform for hosting courses and interacting with students. Here are few features:

- Simple, and quick setup
- Host multiple courses or an entire school
- Create powerful multimedia presentations
- Discussion forums
- Live Chat
- Quizzes (automatically graded)
- Host pre-recorded video/audio lectures
- Build a beautiful landing page to market your school
- Real-time tracking of student progress
- Automated administrative processes like notifications, grading and announcements.

Contact: thinkablelms@gmail.com for more info

Made in the USA
Columbia, SC
11 October 2017